English in Practice

Secondary English Departments at Work

English in Practice

Secondary English Departments at Work

EDITED BY

GEOFFREY SUMMERFIELD

AND

STEPHEN TUNNICLIFFE

CAMBRIDGE

AT THE UNIVERSITY PRESS 1971

Published by the Syndics of the Cambridge University Press
Bentley House, 200 Euston Road, London N.W.1
American Branch: 32 East 57th Street, New York, N.Y.10022

Library of Congress Catalogue Card Number: 78–142129

ISBN: 0 521 07998 5

Printed in Great Britain
at the University Printing House, Cambridge
(Brooke Crutchley, University Printer)

Contents

Contributors

ANTHONY ADAMS: Inspector of Schools for Walsall; Assistant Secretary, National Association for the Teaching of English; formerly Head of the English Department, Churchfields Comprehensive School, West Bromwich.

BRIAN PHYTHIAN: Headmaster, Langley Park School for Boys, Bromley; formerly Head of the English Department, Manchester Grammar School.

ROBERT SHAW: Lecturer, School of Education, Southampton University; formerly Head of the English Department, Leeds Modern School.

IRENE SUMMERBELL: Lecturer in English at the College of St Mark and St John, Chelsea; formerly Head of the English Department, Dane Court Technical High School, Broadstairs.

GEOFFREY SUMMERFIELD: Senior Lecturer in Departments of Education and English, York University; has taught in comprehensive, junior and secondary modern schools and in colleges of education.

STEPHEN TUNNICLIFFE: Head of the English Department, Newtown High School; formerly Head of English, Sowerby Bridge Grammar School.

GRAHAM WHITE: Lecturer in English, Goldsmiths' College, University of London; formerly Head of the English Department, Settle High School.

Introduction

GEOFFREY SUMMERFIELD

This book has a very modest aim: to present an unvarnished account of the way in which several people responsible for English departments in secondary schools conceive and organize their work. It is compiled in response to a need: at a time of the re-organization of secondary schools as institutions and at a time of the reappraisal of English as a subject, many of us are in a state of more or less confusion. Where is coherence and practicality to be found?

Traditionally, the universities and the colleges of education have been the places that one has looked to for guidance and innovation in matters of curriculum: one looked in that direction, because to look in that direction was a matter of custom, of habit, of precedent. But for some time now it has been an open secret that we don't have a great deal to learn from such institutions; both in Britain and in the United States, the colleges of education are too often mere backwaters of lower-middle-class genteelisms, intellectually half-baked and pedagogically hypocritical: the colleges have preached concern for pupils as individuals, but college students showing signs of spirit, that is, of intellectual and social independence, have tended to be branded as members of the awkward squad, and the overall effect of the suburban *mores* and of the cerebral tepidness of the college has been to perpetuate rather flaccid pieties about both life and education. 'Real Life' was somewhere 'out there'.

The history of the colleges has been calamitous: one would never guess so from the professional uniformity of views expressed by the colleges' top brass, but it is clear to anyone with half an eye that most of our colleges represent a retreat from the hurly-burly of the school. Absurdly, the colleges have, in fact, recruited many talented and innovative school-teachers, people of intellectual competence and pedagogical expertise: but the effect of their translation has been to remove them from the 'front line', the place where the real questions are asked and where practical answers have expeditiously to be found. The ensuing separation of some of our most able teachers from the schools, from practical day-to-day involvement in the work of the schools, has been singularly unfortunate: for their influence on the work of the schools has been thereby diminished, to the consequent detriment of the schools and their pupils. Put out to graze in the colleges, the talented teachers of yesterday degenerate with alarming speed into the faintly quizzical, mildly eccentric has-beens of tomorrow, mistily gazing back at the receding battle-fields, compulsively recounting their favourite battle-stories, and occasionally revealing their scars. The departments of education present much the same picture, with the added problem of trying to reanimate students who often need a year merely to recover from the stultifying or traumatic effects of the steeplechase of finals: and too many of their tutors, clinging to a dehydrated liberalism, merely remind one of Noel Annan's comment on John Stuart Mill and Beatrice Webb:

> Perhaps something not entirely pleasant, which artists are quick to sense, emanates from high-minded and dedicated human beings such as Mill and Beatrice Webb. There is a censorious, waspish tone of voice, a lack of sympathy and humour, a contempt for living foolish human beings (as distinct from humanity), an inability to see people except as material to be moulded and exploited, a mind which, if at first open to arguments and facts, closes like a rat-trap once it has digested them—a temperament which in fact is at variance with their creed. [from *The English Mind*, ed. H. Sykes Davies and G. Watson, Cambridge, 1964]

Introduction

It is hardly surprising that relations between the teacher-training institutions and the schools have been strained: the 'higher' institutions wander into a limbo of idealized theorizing, of intellectual self-indulgence, and of snobbish scorn for those who continue to struggle in the schools; while the 'real' teachers grow more puzzled, irritated, or amused by the latest fashions in educational theory that the student teachers bear, unsuspecting and innocent, into the schools during school practice.

The situation is not new, and it has been often enough observed: yet little changes. Too many vested interests are at stake, and it may well be that genuine, radical change will be effected only by the kind of unseemly revolution that has characterized many an American campus in recent months: though, significantly, the teachers' colleges in the United States have been left relatively undisturbed, largely because their students are more rather than less conformist, biddable, well behaved, and 'sensible'.

Fortunately, changes in the teaching of English are being accomplished in a new way, by the teachers in the schools. Such a situation is novel and, I believe, conspicuously healthy. Doubtless the *zeitgeist* will be invoked by way of blanket explanation, but my own inclination is to trace this delightful phenomenon to four main causes.

The first is that many of the best teachers are staying in the schools: in terms of financial reward, the disparities between a teacher in a secondary school and a college of education lecturer are not as wickedly and invidiously great as they were. Secondly, with the spread of comprehensive schools, and the lowering of the average age of teachers in these schools—many quite clearly have a policy of deliberately recruiting younger teachers—the working conditions are better than they were: English departments are seen to require decent provision of room and equipment; heads of departments are less inclined than they were to assume that the only intellectually respectable work is available in work with sixth forms; and the younger teacher is actually allowed to have an opinion about the syllabus and to express it, instead of having to wait for fifteen or twenty years before presuming to have a mind of his own. In the third place, teachers are becoming more autonomous: Sir Alec Clegg's revelations of incompetence and confidence-tricking on the part of the hitherto unaccountable examining boards, and the development of the C.S.E. have both encouraged the teachers to 'presume' to control their own curriculums and examinations. For years, our best English teachers have been teaching well in despite of the examination system—both the selective hurdle at 11+ and the G.C.E. at 15+—and it seems only to have been an undue sense of duty, of responsibility to pupils and parents, that has led them to endure externally operated examinations for so long. It is to be hoped that we go much further in this direction, and much faster, in the next ten years.

Finally, the establishment of curriculum development centres has invited teachers not merely to think about *their own* curricula but also to strive to become more articulate and more accountably articulate about such matters. Significantly, most of these issues are 'political', in that they have to do with power, with who holds the power, with how power is gained, with how power is redistributed: healthily, we are as a profession becoming politically more canny not merely in the sphere of salaries and pensions but—belatedly—in matters of curriculum and examination control. It is in the spirit of these developments in our work, that this volume was conceived and executed: as an offering to a conversation, as data to serve as a basis for a useful comparing of notes, as specific contributions to the current debate about where and how English ought to be moving.

In discussions of innovation and change, matters tend almost inevitably to be piecemeal, fragmentary, isolated, discrete. In showing how certain teachers organize and co-ordinate the work of their departments, this volume may, it is hoped, help others to find their own way of working out problems of progression, of continuity, of order. It may also reinforce the teacher who is tentatively extending the scope and repertoire of his pupils' activities. Consider 'media', for example. The English classroom is still a cinderella: the biologists, chemists, modern language teachers, and many others, have succeeded in wresting from the administrators a decent recognition of their subjects' needs, and enjoy the facilities of purpose-built laboratories. In this matter, the profession of teaching English has simply not yet come of age: what we enjoy is mere 'tokenism', a record-player here, a share of a tape-recorder there. Until we are adequately equipped with technological aides, both of assistants and of equipment, we cannot move our activities in directions responsive to the actively enterprising enthusiasms of our pupils. In the United States, many pupils are fruitfully engaged in experiments in filming, televising, inventive tape-recording, and other similar activities—activities that involve talk, discussion, analysis, appraisal, re-appraisal, collaboration, description, definition, and an extension and a sharpening of language: in such matters, we in Britain have a great deal to learn about the possible roles of our pupils, for example, as I realized when I saw twelve-year-olds at a Maryland Teachers' Workshop teaching their teachers how to make films. I am convinced that, in this respect, the 'training' of teachers needs to become—as soon as possible—much more participatory, much more active, much more synectic, much more creative: the colleges and departments of education need to abandon their lecture-schedules and their Great Books, and set up many more 'workshop' kinds of activities in which tutors collaborate with the students in a series of exemplary activities which can serve as a 'model' for classroom work.

To many American readers, I imagine that this volume's most glaring omission is any sustained attention to sequential work in language, but few of us in Britain are yet prepared to incorporate any kind of systematic grammar or linguistics in our English programmes, though we *are* very willing to learn from the linguists about a proper attitude to dialect or to the subtleties of language-acquisition and -modification. I am sure that we need in the next few years to attend much more carefully, and with a decent sense of urgency, to the findings of socio-linguistics, and specifically to understand the working-class *mores* and non-standard dialects of many of our poorer pupils. Compared with Americans, the British are still crippled by deeply rooted unconscious class-attitudes; just as many lower-middle-class English teachers regard the speech of working-class children as ugly, barbaric, and offensive, so they are also beginning to betray a related cultural chauvinism—the bland notion that Pakistani and Indian children have *no* culture worth attending to. We continue, I'm convinced, to fail most of our pupils from the back streets; and the answer, I'm equally sure, is not to segregate them, either racially or intellectually: such practices are already reaping a bitter harvest, but it may well be that things will have to get worse before we have the humanity, the 'nous', or the desperation, to make them better. The degree to which the traditional curriculum of the school is irrelevant, meaningless, and absurd to many pupils is acknowledged far more openly in the United States than in Britain, even though many American teachers fail, as we do in Britain, to acknowledge the absolute rightness of Malraux's assertion that a *genuine* cultural heritage is not something we are forced to pay respect to but, rather, something that we live by.

It is now admitted by the more perceptive American educationists that the most important recent changes in the high school curriculum have come as a response, not to the challenge of the sputnik, but to the more immediate challenges of the black ghetto. When the school building is burned down, even the most dyed-in-the-wool begin to recognize a need for change, for a move in the direction of life and of recognizing and respecting the lives that the pupils bring to school.

In such matters, it's obvious that transatlantic exchanges of experience and policy can be of great value, so long as we can keep our xenophobia in check: it may now be of use, therefore, to take a brief look at the American high school.

The large high school (with 2,000+ pupils) is the rule rather than the exception; students enter from junior high school at fourteen and stay for four years: at the end, the majority in many such schools go on to college, or university: the academic standards of American colleges and universities are so various and there are so many such institutions, that performance in high school determines not so much whether or not the pupil goes on to tertiary education as which kind of college or university is deemed to be appropriate to his capacities and his vocational intentions.

It is, nevertheless, clear that many American high school English departments consider their job—their selection of curriculum and their methods of teaching—to be largely determined by the college entrance examination. The external pressure on teacher-behaviour is analogous, in this respect, to the influence of British external examinations at O- and A-level of the G.C.E., and the modes of teaching can also be further depersonalized by the size-factor. Pupils in high schools feel themselves to be on a conveyor-belt, and the morale of both pupils and of teachers leaves much to be desired: in this respect, the film, *High School*, directed by Frederick Wiseman, is a source of fascinating first-hand observations: the recurring mode in the classrooms, especially in the humanities, is *instructional*, unrelieved by any active pupil-involvement; and teacher–pupil relations are remarkably distant in a way which one might consider characteristic of the most reactionary British grammar schools.

It is in response to a recognition of these debilities that change is now occurring, in part through the influence of the National Council of Teachers of English, in part through the influence of the 'humanistic psychologists', and in part simply as a response to a sense of impending catastrophe.

N.C.T.E. is clearly committed to change, not for its own sake—as some British xenophobes would argue—but in order to promote English as a humane and humanizing subject: many of its most influential members are not merely concerned that English should be life-enhancing but are actively involved in the dissemination of searching reappraisals, more intelligent curriculum guide-lines, and more relevant and helpful forms of classroom resources.

The influence of the 'humanistic psychologists' is difficult to assess: it stems in part from the work of Abraham Maslow of Brandeis University and Carl R. Rogers of the Western Behavioral Sciences Institute, La Jolla, California, and has aroused heated and occasionally hysterical reactions from conservatives, both political conservatives and moral/pedagogical conservatives. Essentially, it is a means of reinforcing in the individual a sense of what it means to be human: what it means to respond to a person as a *person*, rather than as a 'pupil', or a 'subordinate', or a receptacle: English readers may well see it as related to the kind of insights proposed by Buber's *Between Man and Man*. At root what we have here is a conflict of life-styles, a conflict between those who prefer fluidity, spontaneity of consciousness, openness, a free flow of feeling, on the one hand, and those who stand for stability, the three Rs, strict discipline—law 'n' order—the rugged self-help-style virtues of the frontier and of the right wing of the Republican party: it is a conflict that is both universal and local, a tension that Matthew Arnold examined at length in his analyses of the

Hebraic and the Hellenic in *Culture and Anarchy*, a disparity that John Stuart Mill epitomized in the seminal figures of Coleridge and Jeremy Bentham. In classroom terms, it involves a choice between informality, spontaneity, child-centred activity, and a rigidly preconceived body of knowledge to be efficiently transmitted.

The third factor, the 'sense of impending catastrophe', has to do with the Black Revolution. The gratuitous ugliness and violence of many campus conflicts in recent months is the apparently inevitable legacy of a massive neglect of the black child in the American education system. In the extremer forms of black ideology, one finds a total rejection of white 'supremacist, colonialist' culture: the high school English departments have been too closely geared, in utilitarian fashion, to promoting those ostensible skills which would make high school students acceptable to the colleges and to the employers: in the process, the personal needs of the student were overlooked, and the needs of the 'minority' student in particular were virtually denied. As a result, the drop-out rate of black students has been very high: they have simply 'dropped out' of a school system which attended to the grammar of the standard dialect and to the 'white' official cultural heritage and, in the process, denied the identity of the black person. In such a context, black students were in the position of Ralph Ellison's 'invisible man', and it is hardly surprising that they dropped out. In Britain, if you are in the D stream of a poor secondary modern school, drudging your way through dreary English text-books, you have at least the consolation that the insult of racism is not added unto the injury of third-class status and unrelieved tedium.

In both Britain and the United States, then, the English curriculum in the secondary school is responding to two major pressures, from changes within the subject and from social factors. In some instances, it is impossible usefully to separate these two fields: in the matter of 'correctness', for example, it is clear that we are beginning to see more intelligently the relationship between standard and non-standard dialects, and to accept greater diversity of usage and idiom rather than to expunge deviations from the norm as ruthlessly as may be. In such a question as this, the profession must obviously learn from the psycho-linguists and the socio-linguists: if, then, the reader is disappointed to find here less attention to language-teaching policies than he might have expected, this is due largely to the fact that the departments of linguistics have not yet found an adequate vehicle for the mediation of such findings to the non-specialist teacher. The contributors to this volume were all educated within the mainstream of university 'Eng. lit.' studies: what they know, beyond the range of such studies, they have had to pick up, willy-nilly, by chance, by accident, or by venturing tentatively into the more or less unfamiliar territories of sociology, linguistics, and so on. This seems to me an essential clue to the nature of our present strength and weakness: another crucial clue is that most of us are still trying to catch up with the revolutions in media, both in terms of technical competence—in the management of a cine-camera or a tape-recorder—and in terms of modifying our syllabuses and our day-to-day practices so as to both recognize and use the extensions to the word that such media provide. Similarly, much of this book is a demonstration of the way in which teachers are working to break out of a narrowly conceived notion of their subject, so as to admit, for example, that in our time major artistic talent may well be found in the making of films rather than in the writing of books: but such admissions would clearly lead us to examine and question the persisting narrowness of most university departments of English: and that is another story, and, one trusts, one of our impending controversies.

Meanwhile, it is hoped that this book will serve to dispel

some of the myths propagated by the Black Papers, will serve, that is, to modify such simplistic formulations as depend on root-and-branch dichotomies between 'tradition' and 'progressivism', between conventional wisdom and modish gimmickry; will serve to demonstrate that change is not necessarily change for the worse, and that growth can be accepted as a gradual, intelligently regulated, and ineluctable process. As Cardinal Newman observed, growth is the main symptom of the existence of life.

GEOFFREY SUMMERFIELD

English at Manchester Grammar School

BRIAN PHYTHIAN

Perhaps the most significant change to have overtaken teaching in the last hundred years has been the move towards more child-centred teaching and away from the repressive and paternalistic methods whereby children were regarded, in Dickens's memorable image, as little vessels to be filled up with facts. From the primary schools, whose monopoly of brilliant educational innovation during much of the present century can be partly attributed to their early recognition of the basic rightness of teaching which begins with the child's needs, the change has spread into secondary schools and may even have something to do with current controversies in the universities. Only in recent years have the grammar schools, notably through Nuffield and by audio-visual language teaching, revised their teaching methods, and the lateness of this change is almost certainly connected with the fact that the traditional role of the grammar schools has changed little, as has that of the public schools. This role has been shaped by close ties with the university system, by parental attitudes and career outlets, all of which have remained fairly stable. The whole arrangement has, generally speaking, been thought to work satisfactorily. Certainly the role of Manchester Grammar School, for instance, has changed little since its boarding element disappeared a century ago; at that time its population was established as a mixture of fee-payers and free scholars drawn from a wide area and ultimately going on to the university in large numbers, and this situation persists to the present day. This sort of background, and the only recently conceded respectability of English as a discipline at some universities, still affect, though in a rapidly vanishing way, the teaching of English in long-established grammar schools.

Over a thousand boys from primary and preparatory schools scattered throughout the second largest conurbation in the country sit Part I of the school's entrance examination, though some of these candidates will already have been informally pre-selected for the examination by their head teachers in that weaker candidates will have been discouraged from sitting. The examination, a test of English and mathematics, is set by members of the school staff, and English counts for half of the marks. A smaller number of boys are subsequently recalled for Part II of the examination, which again consists of tests in English and Mathematics, and some 207 are finally admitted to the school. On entry, there is no streaming: the boys are distributed alphabetically among seven forms, pursuing a common curriculum for their first two years in the school; there is virtually no change in the composition of forms for two years. Any rigorous streaming on entry would be superfluous with boys who, it has been suggested, constitute a very narrow ability range, representing perhaps the top five percent of the age-group.

While the school struggles for as long as possible to defer any decisions which may limit a boy's choice of sixth-form or university course—for it is assumed that nearly every boy will enter the sixth form—some adjustments have to be made at the end of the second year, when the seven forms become eight smaller ones. Four of these are devoted to linguistically able boys who add a third language (German, Russian or Greek) to their Latin and French. This increases the number of sixth-form courses available to them, without committing boys to any one course at this stage; however, the choice they make on entering the third form governs their sixth-form career (for example, in so far as a boy opting for Russian will be unable to enter the Classical Sixth). The other forms retain two languages but two of these forms begin a three-year, rather than a two-year, course to O-level. The selection of a third language does not, of course, mean that boys are intending to continue with languages in the sixth form: many boys from the three-language forms enter the Science and Maths Sixths.

Of the 1,450 boys 560 are in one of the four sixth forms. There are small Classical and Mathematical Sixths, and the remainder of the boys divide fairly evenly between the Modern Studies and Science Sixths. A complicated pattern of subjects is offered in the Modern Studies Sixth; suffice it to say that about seventy-five boys are reading for A-level English at any given time, sometimes in sets, sometimes in forms in the case of boys who have chosen a popular grouping such as English, History and French. Partly owing to the youthfulness of many A-level candidates, there is a substantial third-year sixth which includes an English Sixth of about ten boys. Most of these intend to read English at university, and all of them prepare for Oxford and Cambridge scholarship papers, though other potential English undergraduates will have left school after two years in the sixth. In total, between 75 percent and 80 percent of leavers go to universities, and about half of the remainder to other kinds of further education.

No teacher at Manchester Grammar School would wish to say anything that might substantiate the accusation, made frequently by fellow-teachers at conferences or by reviewers of books, that teachers of bright children do not know they are born. To prepare and conduct lessons for volatile youngsters, to mark their copious written work and to help with their multifarious and demanding extra-curricular enthusiasms is quite as wearing as any teaching is, but perhaps in a different way: there is less need for patience, more for stamina, and certainly for a kind of equanimity to modify the recognition that some of one's pupils are brighter than oneself. But there is certainly much in the nature of the school which is specially favourable to education. There is the simple advantage enjoyed by most city schools in the availability of theatres, music, libraries, industries to visit and universities to supply lecturers. There is the fact that boys are literate on entry to the school; they enjoy academic work, and there is no difficulty about persuading them to read widely. The school's ethos, its lack of stuffiness, and its long tradition of welcoming boys from a diversity of home backgrounds ensure that boys from unacademic homes are at no serious disadvantage. Far from being a bastion of middle-class privilege, which Manchester Grammar School is often described as by people who have hardly set foot in the place, the school, if one makes an extrapolation from a recent sample, may draw as many as half of its boys from non-professional backgrounds. It is possible that as boys pass through adolescence, into the sixth form and towards further education, many of them preparing for a social and financial status which only half of them were born into, a lack of parental understanding may become a problem, but in general it is impossible to conclude, from my observation at any rate, that a limited home environment is a significant factor in the education of these able boys.

A school which attracts boys from anything up to twelve miles away, sometimes from farther afield, causing them to commute for an average of about ninety minutes a day, can hardly enjoy close links with its immediate environment: the fragility of such links is part of the price paid for intellectual homogeneity and social catholicity, and, of course, there is much to be said for boys finding some of their friends, their entertainment and their weekend leisure in their home districts. But total separation of school and out-of-school is frankly undesirable if it implies that school ought to be concerned solely with the education of the intellect. Hence our heavy extra-curricular programme, with its special emphasis on camps, treks and expeditions; hence the Service Group, perhaps the first of its kind in the country, with its regional organization and involvement; hence the recently formed Manchester Grammar School Society, already showing signs of regional proliferation in Manchester, and vigorously ensuring that relationships among all those concerned for the school, especially parents, are as firm and personal as possible.

English is taught to every form in the school. Before O-level the allocation is four forty-five-minute periods a week to all forms except the four new three-language third forms, who are reduced to an unsatisfactory three. O-level English language, an examination the crass idiocy of much of which is an appalling testimony to the great gulf which exists between enlightened teachers and some professional examiners, can fortunately be taken in the stride of most forms. Their ability relieves them from practising writing letters to stationmasters, using poetry as comprehension exercises, lifting words out of extracts from dim travel-books into answers, and regarding 'punctuation' as something entirely divorced from the exigencies of self-expression. One wonders how much longer young people will be expected to write essays in forty-five minutes, with no more stimulus than half a dozen words of a title, in circumstances which no writer, not even an instant journalist, would regard as conducive to excellence. In 1970, however, we shall begin participating in the N.U.J.M.B.'s experimental scheme of examining O-level English language by internal assessment and external moderation. As for O-level literature, the fear of having to cope with unsatisfactory set texts by reducing them to knowledge markable in a standardized way causes us to avoid the examination altogether; we prefer to deal with literature *we* have chosen in the light of our own enthusiasms and our assessment of a form's abilities and interests.

In the sixth form, English is taught for three periods a week to scientists and mathematicians, and for two periods to those members of the Modern Studies Sixth who are not reading it for A-level, as part of the non-specialist studies which occupy a third of the sixth-form time-table. Three periods throughout would be preferred, but there is some comfort in the existence of specifically English studies, such as 'the modern novel', 'theatre workshop' and 'creative writing', among the diverse options of 'General Studies'. Again it is fortunate that the 'Test in English' creates no more than a ripple of disturbance: indeed it has been known to impress upon recalcitrant scientists the realization that authority takes non-specialist English seriously!

The English Department consists of ten graduates who teach all but a dozen of the 280 English periods in the school's week, plus a few periods of Games and Divinity. Its members also run the school's termly magazine, the cyclostyled literary magazine, the junior library, the English Society, the Dramatic Society, the Archaeological Society, the annual alpine trek and the school band, and participate in the organization of school teams, camps, societies and the fortnightly printed six-page newspaper. It is a young department, and closely knit: all ten have just finished collaborating on a text-book; three are also working together on a set of course-books, two others on a three-volume series, and one with his brother on a five-volume teaching anthology of poetry. This amount of activity, which has in addition produced six other books in the last three years, is admittedly unusual, but it does give some idea of the number of ideas flying around and of a general air of involvement, experimentation and enthusiasm. If this essay demonstrates nothing else, it ought to indicate that what matters in English teaching is not a system, and certainly not a syllabus, but a number of individuals, dedicated to their work and willing to operate according to their individual talents within a set of broad principles.

There is much cooperation, then, and mutual encouragement, further marked by regular informal gatherings twice a term at the home of one or another of the English masters, providing agreeable opportunities for the exchange of ideas and problems and for that periodic topping-up with enthusiasm that every schoolmaster needs. There are opportunities too, for collaboration: sixth-form practical criticism, English projects for scientists and our new experimental O-level syllabus are some of the topics on which we have produced agreed schemes during the last year or so. All this helps to generate an atmosphere in which every member of the department prefers a personal time-table with a spread of junior, middle and sixth forms, and all have an equal quota of A-level work. Such 'specialists' as there are (and there is no policy of recruiting specialist skills to the department) find sufficient outlet for their particular interests within this pattern (or in general studies) even to the extent that men prefer total responsibility for an A-level group to any system of sharing according to their special interest in an area of work: they place a premium on knowing their pupils by seeing them as much as possible. Despite the complexity of the school time-table, A-level forms can be paralleled to a limited extent to permit team-teaching, but so far this is only in its infancy.

So there is no syllabus, but rather a set of principles attempting to define the spirit in which English should be taught. The basic assumption here is that, in the absence of a body of fact or technique which the English teacher has to pass on, the work must be centred on the individual child, and that what matters most in an experiential situation is the sympathy and liveliness of the individual teacher, who is more likely to be sympathetic and lively if he is choosing his own material and methods and not being required to adhere to those laid down by a head of department who, quite obviously, cannot take into account the individuality of the teacher or that of the particular group of children with whom the teacher has to communicate and whose interests and experience he must understand, synthesize, encourage and guide. More important than the group, however, is that which makes English unique among school subjects: the self-ness of the individual pupil, his awareness of it and of that of others, his active response to thoughts and feelings, and the accuracy of the response. This is the theme, the underlying assumption of all English work in the school, to which this essay will attempt to give expression in practical terms.

Before it is applied to the classroom situation, it may be as well to risk an expansion of it into a more detailed statement of what the aims of English teaching seem to be when applied to able boys who are tolerably well read when they enter the school, who are usually able and willing to talk, and who are going to be in the school for seven years before achieving, ultimately, positions of some responsibility in society. Although for the sake of clarity these aims are isolated from one another in what follows, and may indeed remain separate in a teacher's mind when he is allotting his classroom time, they are all interconnected and overlapping, and no attempt is made to place them in any order of priority: they are, in my view, equally important, and apply throughout the school.

The first aim is to develop the use of the written word with precision, correctness and grace, and since the written word is used for a wide variety of purposes, this means continuous practice in as many types of writing as possible—long and short, prose and verse, imaginative, factual, ratiocinative and narrative. The English teacher's natural bias is towards creative work, for a number of reasons: his own interests, his wish to provide a balance to the academic disciplines of other subjects, and his knowledge that teachers of other subjects will give instruction in the kind of English they wish their pupils to write for them. But if this understandable bias develops into exclusiveness, it damages the pervasiveness of English, another feature of its uniqueness as a subject which gives perspective, coherence and meaning to the whole of the educational process in so far as it ought to develop attitudes, values and a sense of judgement related to the whole of life.

The second aim is to encourage the reading, understanding, appreciation and enjoyment of literature, not as a diffuse activity but as a critical discipline developing standards of value. In addition to deriving all the normal benefits which come from reading verse, stories and drama, the able child can, at quite an early age, be shown the importance of structure and, sometimes, even the nature of style. Again, variety of approach, embracing detailed scrutiny of short pieces in the classroom and broad general reading continuously at home, is part of the recommended pattern, and the process can be said to have failed if a boy leaves school without a love of literature and a capacity to find continuing pleasure in reading and theatre-going.

Spoken English hardly deserves separate mention among this list of aims since it is so obviously a concomitant of a heavy literary emphasis. Neither special practice nor examinations in 'oracy' are likely to become necessary, provided that the tactful correction of slovenly speech, the insistence that reticent boys should not be swamped by the garrulous, and plentiful opportunities for both formal and informal talk, in such contexts as discussion, debate and drama, continue to figure as they do. Regional eccentricities of dialect, incidentally, normally disappear of their own accord before boys leave school, and no teacher would attempt to superimpose 'standard English'.

Finally, a determination to encourage pupils to express themselves, in writing or speech or drama, should not obscure, as it can easily do, the importance of receptivity: the training of intelligent and critical listeners is clearly as vital as that of intelligent writers, readers and speakers, especially in an age dominated by manipulators of mass media where the boundaries of fact, opinion and deliberate untruth are often blurred. The old-style comprehension exercise which required the mechanical transfer of factual material out of a passage and into an answer has rightly been discredited as an arid and unprofitable one; but oral comprehension, memory games, occasional reading to the class, poetry lessons with anthologies closed, and discussions which are organic, not merely a pooling of varied responses, all contribute to training the faculties to absorb critically and to make allowance for other people's ideas provided that they are based on sensible argument or respectable evidence.

Aims, of course, cannot mean anything unless one states what one is aiming at—a topic which deserves a whole book rather than a few sentences. There is space only for a bald assertion: that the aim of such a broad and rich study as has been sketched out is the development in young people of a two fold ability, one having primarily to do with the self, the other primarily with other people, and both ultimately with the greater context of the adult world. The first is the ability to think straight and critically and feelingly, and to express oneself accordingly: here all the various communication skills referred to in the previous paragraphs come together. The second, lest this concern with self-expression should produce mere anarchists or neurotics, is the ability to recognize the relationship between the individual and his society. The need to make the pupil conscious of this relationship (a familiar part of the definition of education as a 'preparation for life') has sometimes in schools been made an excuse for religious propaganda or for an insistence on types of secular conformity (in dress, for example); on a wider scale it may puzzle those teachers who are reluctant to declare their own interpretation of the values, traditional or emergent, of society. Surely literature has a key role here, in that it can make the pupil more fully aware that a wide range of interpretations is available.

These two abilities correspond roughly to two of the needs of adult society: a degree of individuality and a degree of conformity. The former is satisfied by maximizing the degree of child-centredness in English teaching, by aiming at fully developed (which means fully communicating) individuals. The latter is assisted by ensuring that English, and especially literature, is conceived as a liberal and humane discipline which will, in part, familiarize youngsters with the life of the society they belong to. This notion represents a broadening of what has previously been described as the themes of this essay—the concern of English with the self-ness of the individual—because I do not see how any definition of 'self-ness', 'child-centred' or the like can fail to include a reference to the self-ness of other people, human nature being what it is. So there is, by this definition, no incompatibility between a stress on the child-centredness of English and a recognition of the subject's social responsibilities.

This statement of principles has already glanced at classroom practice, and before a fuller documentation of such practice at various levels—junior and middle school, A-level and non-specialist sixth-form work—it is perhaps worth reiterating the interdependence of these several aims by describing what I would regard as a central feature of English teaching at all levels of the school. It is based on the belief, which only O-level examiners appear to dissent from, that a desire to express oneself cannot be separated from having something to say, and that the teacher's responsibility is therefore to ensure that no pupil is ever expected to write *in vacuo*—except when practising instant composition for examination purposes. With able pupils, literature is the most obvious source of stimuli, for not only does its content, duly digested and discussed, provide starting-points for the pupils' own self-expression, but also its form and style—be it a piece of rhythmic verse, a closely reasoned argument, a slangy anecdote—give the pupils a suggested (but not ordained) structure for their work.

In practice, this means that, say, a piece of verse, carefully selected in the light of the form's maturity and ability, is first discussed in a conventional way. The most obvious talking-point will be the nature of the experience embodied in the poem, and a consideration of this will involve pupils in responses which will include some reference to their personal and collective experience, feelings, attitudes and thought-processes: these responses will interpret the poem and, in turn, be clarified by it in a way which ought to be exciting and provocative, assuming that the teacher is doing his job discreetly and creatively. And if this discussion is properly conducted, by teacher or by pupils, there ought to emerge a realization, however rudimentary, of something of the function of shape, movement and imagery in the poem, though clearly there will be a difference between the first-former's apprehension of, for instance, 'comparisons' or 'word-pictures', and the sixth-former's grasp of 'symbol'. Equally clearly, there is a legitimate difference of opinion between teachers who believe that young children should be taught the meaning of regular rhythm *before* they can understand the feel of free-moving verse well enough to write it themselves, and those who discourage children from writing in metre because of the padding and the laceration of grammar which they fall back on. But however the teacher interprets his task, it remains true that the discussion of poetry can, and ought to, get away from the paraphrase of extractable 'meaning' towards a consideration, albeit sketchy, of the wholeness of a poem, including its technique. Let us assume, however, that the teacher gets this far, and finally pushes the exercise to its logical conclusion by encouraging pupils to write their own verse, perhaps modelled on the subject matter or form of the poem they have been discussing, perhaps not—for it is extremely useful to offer able pupils a choice in the degree of structuring which the teacher offers.

In such a process, many of the faculties of the pupils have been brought into play, and due attention has been paid to both individual and group work. The pupils have read literature, talked about it in an attempt to understand it and relate it to their own experience, listened to other people's reactions, perhaps thereby deepening their own, and finally focused the whole to a satisfying conclusion. This kind of approach, which can equally well be applied to prose, recorded drama and, *mutatis mutandis*, visual stimuli, such as photographs, harmonizes the various aims of English in a way which gives them discernible point and direction, and has sufficient flexibility and scope for variety to justify, I hope, the earlier claim that it can be regarded as a core-activity in English teaching. Additionally, of course, one hopes that pupils will be able, or rather willing, to write about what they see and feel without this amount of underpropping, but it is for the teacher to decide how and when the degree of structuring can be gradually modified as the pupils move up the school.

In the younger forms (to embark now on a chronological review) teaching conditions are at their most favourable; subsequently one may have to cope with inhibiting factors ranging from adolescence to public examinations, from the smaller number of periods in the sixth form to the mistaken notions of 'specialization' and the damnable connotations of 'minority time' which cause some senior boys to regard English as peripheral. During the early years, however, receptivity and enthusiasm are at their most conspicuous, and the teacher has the opportunity to lay out the whole range of English work in a full and pleasurable way.

The kind of creative exercise already described accounts for much of the time, including the weekly assignment of written homework, the return of which provides occasion not only for a valuable post-mortem but also for what little teaching of formal grammar is necessary. The latter is only dealt with publicly if there are general faults: otherwise it is explained privately—in 'surgeries' which are held as often as the rest of the form are busied with other work, such as large-scale group projects on preparing a piece of drama, a committee-report or a radio programme. (Creating opportunities for 'surgeries' significantly taxes the ingenuity of any teacher who makes a point of giving personal attention.) Correct grammar is, after all, only an aid to expression, and the first priority would seem to be to get the words flowing as a necessary preliminary to making the pupil realize for himself the usefulness of the aid. The teacher judges the extent to which individual pupils can tolerate the recrimination of red ink, and a good case can be made out for distinguishing between imaginative work, as an occasion rather for a comment than for lavish correction or even a mark, and shorter pieces, or work into which the pupil has put less of himself, as occasions for more rigorous emphasis on precision. All this is not to deny the importance of high standards of technical accuracy, or of an insistence that words ought not be be used sloppily, but merely to draw attention to priorities: a pupil who has aimed at spontaneity, freshness, acuteness of observation and fidelity to experience is unlikely to be encouraged if his work comes back with every misplaced comma blighted by the teacher.

This respect for individual growth, difficult as it is to sustain in forms of thirty, can be extended to other lessons, such as those which deal with literature *per se*, if the teacher can continue to reconcile himself to the fact that self-discovery by the pupil is likely to prove as memorable as, and often more memorable than, instruction by the teacher. This is now generally accepted as far as drama is concerned: the shortage of good printed plays for junior forms has helped to promote improvised drama, and no one who has seen the intense involvement of even the most sophisticated children in imaginative play can doubt its value as a legitimate means of self-expression and -exploration, though it is not always easy to persuade staider colleagues, and the school doctor, that there is more than an accidental relationship between respectable education and the cheerful informality of a drama session. Perhaps this is a useful moment to digress into an occasional, though not a serious, problem which arises from a point made at the beginning of this essay, where reference was made to schools in which teaching-methods have only recently stopped being traditional. The time has passed when it was considered daring to move desks about or take children out of the formroom into the open air, or when a German teacher could complain that it was the business of English teachers to instruct children in the difference between strong and weak verbs. Many subjects have now revised their teaching-methods to bring them broadly into line with what enlightened English teaching long ago proclaimed: that education is just as much a matter of drawing out as of putting in. But there still remain traces of subject-valuation by tangible results: in the dog-fight for more periods in the middle school, for example, a head of department who can point to an increase in the amount of knowledge required by the O-level examiners has, understandably enough, an advantage over one who can only champion the intangibles. And pity the many teachers of English who have to live with the bone-headed traditional respect for hard-edged disciplines which is exemplified in Robin Davis's *The Grammar School* (Penguin Books, 1967): in the course of an apologia for Latin, he fends off the rival claims of English by stating that the English 'pundits' cannot even agree what English is. 'Some stress mundane matters of spelling and punctuation...' (who, one would like to know?) '...others precision in writing, others depth of comprehension, others wealth of literary experience and so on.' His conclusion is predictable. Presumably he would be even more baffled if he knew that some of us believe English to be all of these, and a good deal more besides, and moreover succeed in implementing this belief in at least one school not noted for indifferent academic standards.

Improvised drama can, if it avoids the familiar traps of shapeless emoting and undisciplined exhibitionism, bring with it some understanding of basic theatrical skills and conventions and this will stand pupils in good stead when they come to study printed drama in the two or three years before O-level. But the availability of printed plays at this level ought not to induce total formality in drama lessons. Manchester Grammar School is fortunate in having its own theatre, as it is in having a junior library and an increasing number of classrooms furnished in a way which is favourable to small-group discussion and writing projects. The school's development plan also makes provision for a much needed recording and play-back studio, to do away with the abysmal humping of electronic machinery down long corridors into unsatisfactory rooms. Such facilities, which of course are rapidly becoming standard features in secondary schools, help to ensure that the formality of 'reading round the class' (which can kill the dramatic impulse) is supplemented by the tape-recorder, the record-player and the acting area—by living drama, in fact.

In the absence of good printed plays for junior forms, the main exposure to literature comes from weekly attention to poetry and the class-reader (not read round the class, either), discussed, acted, dramatized for radio, or otherwise more fully absorbed. At the same time the pupil's own private reading is constantly encouraged, brought out into the open in lecturettes or short readings, or even talked about at the lunch-table or in the corridors—anything to foster personal attention, individual growth, and that sense of trust between teacher and pupil without which little of real worth in English teaching can be accomplished.

Perhaps something of the pattern of junior- and middle-school teaching is now emerging. At the centre is that synthesis of reading, understanding, talking, writing and, after homework, commentary on the writing. Equally continuous, preferably weekly, is the enjoyable experience of a diversity of drama, prose and poetry, increasing in depth as the sixth form is approached. Peripherally, debates, personal anthologies, records of private reading, form magazines, theatre-visits and projects all represent further explorations and statements of experience. I myself encourage all my junior forms to keep a daily journal which is intended to be a work-book or source-book of ideas, incidents, thoughts and observations (in prose or verse) which may subsequently be useful in more formal contexts. A similar emphasis on immediacy of response and precision of expression is found in regular sessions of what has been called 'intensive writing'—off-the-cuff reactions (perhaps polished later) to visual or auditory stimuli produced in the classroom or found out of doors—enough to provide material for a couple of detailed paragraphs; thus something special can be made out of something ordinary, even by the child who normally 'can't think of anything to say'.

The teacher is given no lists of prescribed books for his forms: there is departmental agreement that certain books are more suitable for one year group than another, but this is simply to ensure that the third-form teacher whose class is drawn from half a dozen second forms can guarantee to find something that none of them has yet dealt with. (Though the school is far from wealthy, it wisely refuses to regard the supply of books as a fit area for economy.) Neither is there any attempt to make sure that all forms in any given year do the same sort of work: while one fourth form is cutting its way through piles of newspapers to produce group-reports on newspaper attitudes or advertising methods, another one in the next room may be listening to a tape-recording of *Macbeth* or a B.B.C. broadcast on war poetry. It may not be a system which appeals to the tidy-minded. Like all education, it is an act of faith: partly of faith that teachers will be able to hold all this diverse activity in a meaningful focus by the strength and sensitivity of their personalities and by their sense of values; principally of faith that pupils, by the interaction of what they are and what they are confronted with, will enter the sixth form not only able to write accurately, talk articulately and understand carefully, but also with disciplined minds and feelings as a foundation on which to build a maturer capacity for discrimination and judgement.

Teaching English to A-level raises issues which differ only very little from those raised in other schools at this level. The age of the boys is sometimes a problem: because most of them take O levels after four years, they have to come to terms with A-level prescribed texts at the age of sixteen, or even earlier, and though most of them have the intelligence to cope, not all have the worldly experience or emotional range which would help them to penetrate more deeply into certain of the texts, especially the compulsory Shakespeare plays which often include one or two mature tragedies. In a sense, of course, any understanding of a mature Shakespeare play is bound to be less than total, at any age, but those schools whose pupils have the benefit of being twelve months older are at an advantage, for twelve months during adolescence is perhaps a longer time, in terms of widening understanding and quickening responses, than a year in later life. Another factor which works against entirely satisfactory English teaching at this level is one which, in fact, applies to all boys' schools, and indeed to all single-sex schools: the lack of members of the opposite sex whose responses, pooled in seminar conditions, make for a more totally rounded group understanding of a piece of literature.

The answer to both these problems is one which has achieved widespread educational respectability in recent years: the tailoring of public examinations to the circumstances of individual schools by those people who are in the best position to understand those circumstances, namely the teachers.

To inveigh against the shortcomings of yet another examination would be to invite accusations of being predictable and would go over territory already fully explored more authoritatively. But a brief complaint is necessary, partly because the antipathy of English teachers to the present English examinations has not yet succeeded in making the slightest impression on the only examining board I am competent to write about, and partly because it is impossible to write about English teaching for A-level without some reference to the examination which consummates it. Briefly, then, the examination is a bad one because the candidates are required to answer a total of eight questions, only one of which is an unseen passage for criticism, and the rest of which, on the set texts, are answerable by the regurgitation of 'opinions' (Frank Whitehead's 'ficts') which may give no evidence whatsoever of the perceptiveness of the candidate. Examiners' reports annually lament stereotyped, second-hand answers in terms which suggest that the examiners quite fail to realize that the solution is in their own hands. Meanwhile in many schools teachers continue to take the easy way out: they know that a mere pass is now no longer sufficient for entrance to the arts side of a university; they are frequently under pressure to 'get good results'; they often find themselves teaching pupils who have been selected for the A-level examination not because of their literary ability but because the time-table requires certain groupings of subjects and it is sometimes assumed that 'anyone can do English'—which, of course, is true so long as English is equated with the memorization of 'ficts'.

It is not always easy to persuade pupils that matters regarded by the examiners as of no consequence (creative writing, wide general reading, a willingness to talk) must nevertheless figure in English work, but constant pressure by teachers can cause these matters to receive their rightful due of attention. A possibly specious relevance, but for anxious or ambitious candidates a reassuring one, can be given to some creative writing by finding stimuli in whatever literature is currently under consideration, but under ideal circumstances, which only teachers can create by their own attitudes and approach, creative writing should go forward all the time to give boys a continuing opportunity to come to terms with themselves and their environment as well as to provide them with first-hand insight into creative processes. Wide general reading can also be related to set texts, and in an increasingly examination-conscious situation it may have to be tested to make sure it has been done, but again the onus is on the teacher to create an attitude of mind which regards continuous reading as something other than an examination-orientated chore. In fact the whole notion of teaching *for* A-level is infamously short-sighted unless it includes teaching for *beyond* A-level, equipping the pupil with interests and skills, enthusiasms and sensibilities, which he will retain for the rest of his life, or at least long after the 'ficts' have, like their brother facts, been deservedly forgotten.

So long, then, as the examination which concludes the A-level course fails to take account of some activities which most of us would regard as an indispensable part of English work, and does not even place at its own centre a basic critical activity by the pupil, the teacher has to make certain that various principles figure prominently in his programme. Some of these have already been referred to: the importance of creative writing; the need for wide general reading as a necessary basis for the making of literary judgements; and, above all, informing all others, the spirit of enquiry and enjoyment, the creation of a sense of values which transcends the mere requirements of A-level. Other important issues remain, among them the place of literary history and the role of practical criticism.

To the question 'How are these principles implemented?' there is again no clear answer, and certainly no simple system to be recommended. In the informality of the seminar or the tutorial, confronted by a small number of pupils, the teacher is even more dependent on his enthusiasms, even more thrown back on the resources of his own temperament, and even more exposed in a dynamic person-to-person situation than he is lower down the school. (And how convenient it is to have at one's disposal rooms furnished with tables and chairs—a far more valuable innovation than one could foresee—which can be arranged in a way conducive to seminar rather than lecture; not to mention a working atmosphere in which tutorials can be held while the rest of the form are profitably employed elsewhere.) This essay has already stressed that the teacher is more important than the syllabus. All that can be done here is to describe an approach and to insist yet again that what matters most is the spirit and flexibility with which individual teachers present it.

A cardinal feature of this approach is to delay work on the set texts for as long as possible. In practice, this means that the first two terms in the sixth form are devoted to a general introductory course, unless an early assessment of a form's ability, or the presence among the compulsory set texts of a long or specially difficult work, such as *King Lear*, makes it necessary to make an earlier start on the texts (a pity, because these are precisely the circumstances in which a *longer* introductory course is needed). A concentrated course in practical criticism is placed towards the beginning, on the grounds that the terms of criticism should be redefined, for convenience's sake, as soon as possible. This is not expounded as an 'open sesame', but permitted to grow out of a general discussion of pieces, mainly verse, selected and graded carefully to confront pupils with the main issues: an obvious emphasis here is never to permit the technique of criticism to obscure the value of literature as a total experience. Once pupils have learnt to structure their responses verbally, and set them down on paper in an orderly fashion, the tools of criticism are kept sharp by continuous exercise, on the sort of material which is generally found in A-level papers, and subsequently on the set texts. Most of us would regard this critical work as the central binding feature of the A-level programme.

It would also be generally agreed, I think, that the introductory course should try to give students some feeling for the overall shape of English literature, partly to structure a subject which some boys find uncomfortably vague in comparison with more hard-edged subjects, partly to provide a context for the set texts, which our board does not group in any way, and partly to indicate the organic nature of literature and the relationship between individuals and their cultural contexts. The pre-Elizabethan background is best apprehended through a glance at the history of drama; subsequently, the fact that poetry has a more continuous history suggests that a swift gallop through English verse is the best way of pointing out the main periods. The study of post-Shakespearian drama is concentrated on the modern period, with the emphasis on 'aspects of the theatre' rather than on reading whole plays in class—a time-wasting and frequently unedifying practice. It is a programme which could easily become confusing and superficial, and an even greater danger is the temptation to produce a body of knowledge about literature, but with care and judicious selection of material it can be made to work.

These, then, are the central features of the introductory course, and the teacher fits in his other priorities at his convenience: creative writing, constant encouragement to keep up general reading, occasional riding of hobby-horses (the mass-media, the definitions of culture) and perhaps the odd half-hour of improvised drama or a free-for-all on censorship when the going is getting heavy. Although as time progresses the focus will narrow, the subject matter become more heavily literary, the teaching more confined to talk, there is no need to regard the step into the sixth form as irrevocably leaving behind the diversity of content and method which characterized middle-school teaching.

The same is true of set texts. The pressure of time and the exigencies of the examination tend to produce, for much of the remaining four terms of the sixth-form course, stereotyped lessons in which students pore over the texts, the garrulous few contribute, the majority remaining silent, while the teacher may rely on the inspiration of the moment to replace intensive preparation and interesting presentation of the material. Here, yet again, is a problem for the individual teacher's sense of what basically he is about, and if he lifts his eyes often enough to contemplate what his pupils are likely to be *after* the exam, he will surely spend as much time as he can in devising lively lessons, and not allow himself to lapse into the quiet brooding which sometimes passes for teaching at, say, the university.

Finally, there remains the problem of teaching English to non-specialists in the sixth form, and now one is tempted to go immediately on to the defensive and start apologizing for the fact that mathematicians are likely to resent having to spend time on a subject they have chosen not to pursue into the sixth form because they may be no good at it, and that scientists cannot be persuaded to see the relevance of English to the harassing business of getting through A-levels and into a university. Sales-resistance is only slight at Manchester Grammar School, and exists hardly at all among the brighter forms, who could probably have joined the Modern Studies Sixth anyway, had they wanted to, and who are clever enough to have time and intellectual energy to spare. But where it does exist, is it not possible that the teacher is at fault as much as the boys? For the entirely understandable reason that he is heavily worked, he may put his non-specialist sixths at the bottom of his list of priorities when thinking up bright ideas for lessons and finding time for marking. And so boys' apathy may simply be a reflection of the teacher's, in the uncanny way that boys have of sometimes understanding the teacher better than he does himself.

This question of work-load is worth closer scrutiny. Even with our short working-day, short because of the amount of commuting that boys have to do, a teacher confronts classes for about twenty hours a week. Quite apart from the energy dispensed during these hours, the amount of preparation, especially for A-level, is enormous, and the average amount of marking per week includes three sets of marking from junior forms, a set of up to seventeen three-hour essays from A-level candidates, and whatever writing is produced by up to three non-specialist groups per teacher. It is quite clear that even if the teacher marks during all his free periods (instead of collecting his wits) and every afternoon after school (instead of running a society or sports team), he will still have to spend two or three entire evenings a week on preparation and marking, even before he starts thinking of his own private reading —or his family and social life. The situation is made no easier by the knowledge that if he took a job in a college of education, teaching to the same level, he would earn considerably more for about half the amount of teaching and preparation and a quarter of the amount of marking. It is certain that a case can be made out for reducing the teaching-load of teachers in some subjects.

But the scientists and mathematicians, of course, deserve as much of the English master's attention as any other boys in the school. They have a syllabus heavily loaded with fact-learning, not always with a heavy emphasis on the development of ideas, and this may produce a narrow view not only of science but of life itself. Their lessons in English will be the last formal occasion when non-scientific reading and writing will be required of these university entrants and future citizens, and the last occasion when there will be someone appointed to encourage them to think about something other than their degree subjects and their jobs. For both these reasons, quite apart from his wish to teach his subject successfully, the English teacher ought to regard these forms as demanding special qualities of care, patience and persuasiveness.

If English has been taught with vigour, variety and relevance in the lower school, and if the school has a well established system of non-specialist studies in the sixth form, the teacher will find his difficulties lessened, especially if he regards sixth-form studies as a continuation of earlier work, and sixth-formers as post-O-level boys, not as some new kind of 'specialist' enemies determined to reject English as not pertinent to the technological nirvana. When all is said and done, what principally matters in teaching these boys is what matters elsewhere: establishing a right relationship within the group, and then proceeding on the assumption that no antipathy exists.

If it does exist, it is worth taking the antipathy as a starting-point for the course, and discussions (not assertions) about the value of English periods often lead to a valuable examination of the important and wide-ranging issues implied in the clichés used by young scientists on the offensive. Alternatively there is a good case for starting with the thoughts and feelings that matter to young scientists, discussing scientific method, the importance of fact-finding, of logical thought and accurate expression, and moving outward to scientifically-based subjects which have a wide bearing: the effects of science on biological evolution; the increasing domination of environment; mass production and its consequent mass persuasion techniques. This latter leads naturally to a discussion of language used for purposes other than the communication of fact, and opens up fields of work having to do with politics, the press, and entertainment generally. From popular culture it is only a short step to the serious arts. This approach has the advantage of involving the scientist at many points, and should further the development of logical reasoning in speech and writing; at the same time the sixth-former is being made critically aware of the world around him. All this doubtless involves the teacher in familiarizing himself with scientific history and method, but why not? It is highly unlikely that a watered-down A-level course will suit these boys, and the successful teacher at this level is more likely to be not the one who stands aloof from the scientist's preoccupations and beckons towards his own pinnacle, but the one who, recognizing the extent to which science has mattered and does matter in civilization, uses his pupils' interest in this subject to extend their range of experience, concern and discrimination, and their ability to express themselves orally and on paper.

There is no reason, of course, why such a plan should not also be followed with boys on the arts side who are not taking English as a specialism; it probably will be followed by those teachers who are concerned about the development of a 'two-cultures' feeling in school. This area of work is made no easier by the allocation of only two periods of English a week to the Modern Studies Sixth, on the assumption that these boys are additionally exposed to the humanities in their specialist subjects (they have two periods of science, too). Since a very drastic pruning of priorities is thus made necessary in planning an English programme for such boys, it is probably best to retain that area of English which is unique to the subject, namely the literature, and cut out everything else, rather than run the risk of attaining diversity at the price of superficiality. Sometimes the scope of such a literary course can be widened by tying in non-specialist English with specialist A-level studies, and deepening the understanding of, for instance, a period of history by looking at its literature. Similarly, with the co-operation or at the request of a teacher of Modern Languages or Classics (both of which have little to do with literary studies as they are understood by English specialists) a course in practical criticism, or tragedy, or a special project (such as a documentary treatment of the death of Socrates) can be profitable. A good case can also be made out for binding together 'general studies' in a meaningful pattern, rather than merely offering a collection of miscellaneous options which reflect the personal enthusiasms of members of staff. Thus a synoptic view of the Elizabethan period, to take an obvious example, can be provided by teachers of English, Music, Art, Science and History working together. All these patterns have been tried with success, except for the last one, which is currently impossible because General Studies are taken in sets grouped according to the sixth-formers' choice, while English is taught by forms. Once again, the diversity of patterning exists because of the autonomy of English teachers and because they are allowed to tailor their courses to suit the needs of their particular groups.

It will now be apparent that whatever philosophy and whatever method of English teaching have emerged from this review of the practice of one school derive from the characteristics of its English Department: a responsible graduate staff, creative relationships among them and with other departments, pupils whose development can be encouraged over a long period, and a concern for pupils' individual growth. It is this last-mentioned which gives rise to most unresolved problems, and which ought to be the subject of the most important thinking about English teaching in the next few years: how to reconcile, in practice, individual attention and large classes, so that personal collaboration between teacher and pupil can replace, for some of the time at least, the traditional and still current over-emphasis on mass teaching.

One final point, still on this question of 'thinking about English teaching'. The English teacher has already been sketched as a man burdened with preparation and marking. Picture him also trying to keep abreast with *The Times Educational Supplement* and other educational periodicals, *The Use of English*, National Association for the Teaching of English bulletins, conferences, local branch meetings, National Short Courses, one-day schools, lectures, Schools Council Working Papers, examination board reports, surveys, research, books about teaching, publishers' catalogues, linguistics, programmed learning, oracy, or whatever else the education departments throw up. Bemused and despairing, the English teacher needs something else, something more than secondary reorganization, more, even, than the expenditure of money on his own school department. He needs a place where he can go away and think: a national staff college of English, to which he can be seconded for a term at regular intervals, so that he can periodically evaluate his function and recharge his batteries. In no other subject is a teacher's vitality, freshness and sense of direction more important, and we give insufficient thought to their care.

It may be complained that the aims of English teaching as outlined in this essay are very wide, perhaps nearly as wide as those of education itself. If this is so, there is an explanation. Part of the educational process is concerned with equipping young people for 'life' (an unsatisfactory term, but meaningful enough in this context). In so far as English is concerned with communication, without which much of life would be inconceivable, and with literature, which has a habit of being coexistent with life, the preoccupations of English and those of education generally are clearly related. To practise communication is to define the communicator, his experience of life, and the relationship between the two. To study literature is to absorb and evaluate aspects of life: both communication and literature, therefore, represent for the pupil a coming to terms with an enlarging world which is gradually becoming synonymous with the world of the adult citizen. Hence the centrality of English in much of primary and secondary education. It may also be complained that the aims of English out-lined in this essay are *too* wide, impracticably so. But if a school which believes it has the potential and the will to be a centre of excellence cannot aim high at the ideal of the cultured man, who can?

Re-shaping the English syllabus at Newtown High School

STEPHEN TUNNICLIFFE

Newtown High School is a Welsh country comprehensive school of 800 plus. Lying in a thinly-populated and still depopulating area, it escapes some of the difficulties and pressures of the bigger city comprehensive schools, but has others peculiar to itself, as a brief outline of its development will show.

Before the pressure towards comprehensive secondary schooling made itself felt, the educational system in Montgomery followed the usual pattern of small single-sex grammar schools, and amorphous mixed secondary moderns—usually the old elementary schools 'developed'. In Newtown there was also a junior technical school. A far-sighted director of education recognized the possibilities of secondary re-organization in the area and pressed, while money was still freely available, for new secondary school buildings throughout the county. As a result the secondary schooling now is organized in six small comprehensive schools—the largest being under 1,000—all housed in comparatively new buildings.

In Newtown the reorganization can be summarized thus:

BEFORE RE-ORGANIZATION

(*a*) Boys' grammar school of approximately 150 pupils; girls' grammar school of approximately 150 pupils. These two schools, under separate heads, were housed together in one building. They accounted for some 30–40 percent of the school population.

(*b*) Pen-y-Gloddfa modern school, mixed. This was the old elementary school developed.

(*c*) The junior technical school.

FIRST PLAN

A combined co-educational grammar school for Newtown and its neighbour Welshpool, to be built mid-way between the two. The existing modern and technical schools in Newtown would then have been developed separately. (After initial development this was abandoned as impracticable in view of travelling distances involved. It has a bearing on the present school, in that the building was designed as the new technical school.)

SECOND PLAN

(*a*) 1958. Children from Pen-y-Gloddfa joined the boys' and girls' grammar schools, still under separate heads, but in the present building (then just completed).

(*b*) 1964. On retirement of the respective heads the two schools were amalgamated under a newly appointed headmaster (formerly headmaster of a superseded secondary modern school in Welshpool). Between these dates the junior technical school ceased to be used for secondary education, and was developed as a college of further education. It had already served some of the functions of one, with day-release and vocational courses.

This pattern of re-organization has led to certain features of the present comprehensive school, which is beginning to evolve an identity of its own—the progress in that direction is noticeable year by year. On the whole it has been a sensible practical development. The former grammar schools, by virtue of being housed together, did in fact already possess many co-educational features. They were fortunate, too, in their heads, who were able to work fairly harmoniously in spite of considerable differences of personality. The present school staff still includes members from the secondary modern, the grammar and the junior technical schools, in whom the sense of identity with the new school has successfully absorbed differences of approach. The transition has in fact been accomplished without the violent and unproductive demands for re-adjustment made on teachers by more rapid and radical plans, and Newtown is fortunate in having escaped the more lunatic consequences of doctrinaire comprehensivization in the form of single-school complexes housed in buildings miles apart, which forms an unhappy feature of the comprehensive system in other parts of Wales.

The development of the school has been along cautiously liberal lines. The lack of cohesion inevitable in a 'compounded' comprehensive school of this type has not been countered by any vigorous single-minded pursuit of specific aims. In common with many new schools, in fact, it has lacked dynamism, and there has been too much casting round for currently acceptable lines of development. As long as schools—especially over the appointment of staff—are actively controlled and restricted by local governing bodies largely ignorant of, and indifferent to, the long-term aims of education and their practical interpretation in the classroom, this state of affairs will persist. Educational advances will tend to come from the piecemeal and unco-ordinated efforts of individual teachers.

At Newtown this tendency is aggravated in two ways: the small town community being relatively self-contained and isolated, there are often undue local pressures influencing the governors which a headmaster owing his own appointment to them finds it hard to resist. Where everyone knows everyone else, talent tends to be obscured by familiarity, and judgement distorted, especially by local political affiliations. Secondly, as might be expected in a small school, the post of deputy head is already regarded as a spring-board to promotion—the first two lasted just two years each, long enough to assess the situation and begin to initiate new policy, but not long enough to carry anything through. Investigation into the deleterious effects of such an approach to 'administration'—the term already has an unsavoury aura of business efficiency that is quite alien to true educational ideals—lies outside the present study, but I suspect it will become increasingly pressing over the next few years, as small comprehensives multiply, where any shedding of the teaching load by the 'administrators' is directly felt as an increased burden by the rest of the staff. One can detect in staff-rooms a growing cynicism as to what 'they' —the administrators at the top—will busy themselves with next, and this can lead at worst to an irresponsibility—'Let them worry, they're paid for it!'—that does nothing but harm, intensified as it is by the present invidious pay-structure in the profession.

Before examining the English work more closely, some further comment is necessary on certain features peculiar to Newtown High School.

In the first place, there is the effect of its being Welsh. Newtown is not in a strong Welsh-speaking area—only 7 percent of school pupils are native Welsh speakers—nor one in which there are strong nationalist tendencies. Indeed, its history as the centre of a thriving woollen industry in the nineteenth century, drawing its expertise from outside the country, has tended the other way. There has always been a strong English element in the local population, and the need for any ambitious person to speak English has in the past devalued the Welsh language locally. Recently the establishment of small industries with outside capital has maintained the trend, and one can detect some prejudice against the 'native' tongue amongst pupils and parents. This is not lessened by the fact that Welsh is compulsory in the first three years at school, and that the artificial promotion of Welsh teaching loads the time-table and staff allocations to the detriment of other language studies. It is interesting to observe in connection with this that only three of the graduate staff have degrees from English universities, and almost half the staff speak Welsh. In spite of this, under the re-organization of secondary education many of the Welsh-speaking children were directed away from Newtown itself so as to concentrate them in schools serving a more Welsh catchment area. The few we do get find difficulties initially, but tend to overcome them by about the third year. No special provision is made for extra English teaching.

Secondly, the nature of the physical environment needs a word or two. The area is a rural one, with farming and forestry still the most important industries. The farms are mostly small, and life on them is often primitive by present-day standards. Under a new scheme for rural development in Mid-Wales small and uneconomic farms are now being combined to form larger units, and the committee has compulsory purchase powers when needed. Nevertheless, the local farmers can at present only rarely absorb the labour of their own children, and any ambitious or able pupils tend to look farther afield for their career. There are one or two small firms (plastics and engineering), and plans are in hand for the expansion of Newtown to about twice its present size over the next ten years. This has not been enough to exert pressure for vocational courses on any scale at the school, the college of further education providing these. Discussions are now in progress over the enlargement of the school; the authority plans to combine the new building required for R.S.L.A. with the first phase of an expansion programme aimed at adapting the school to accommodate about 1,500 pupils.

Perhaps because Newtown lacks the prosperity of an industrial area the school is truly comprehensive in its social range, catering for all but one or two secondary pupils in its scattered catchment area. There is no creaming off, either to grammar schools (which no longer exist in the county) or to status-promoting fee-paying schools. Indeed, we occasionally accept into the senior school pupils who have been transferred from fee-paying schools, who are attracted by the wider range of subjects available. The school is thus in a favourable position to make the most of comprehensive education. It was for this reason that I came to the school, and with this in mind that I have attempted to re-shape the approach to English here.

The sixth form at Newtown has grown slowly to its present size of about seventy (i.e. 9 percent of the school population), but is still seen chiefly as material for an A-level course on grammar-school lines, with little provision for General Studies, or for the impending changes in senior work. I have prepared a scheme for an integrated General Studies course (see Appendix) which should do something to rectify this. It has had the enthusiastic support of most senior teachers and came into effect in September 1968. I believe such a team method—no more than already operates in many schools—is the most fruitful line for development at Newtown, and that it could lead to more radical curriculum reform in the direction of integrated subject syllabuses. I see my own English syllabus as an interim step in that direction.

The school has at present a six-form intake. The class/streaming system has undergone some experimentation over the last two or three years. The intention has been to establish classes of mixed ability, grouping them according to district, and teaching some non-academic subjects to these unstreamed groups. This plan is still followed, but is showing the need for some modification owing to the difficulties (*a*) in determining how to ensure a truly unstreamed group without adequate guidance from the primary schools; (*b*) in reconciling the district grouping principle (whose validity is in any case doubted by many staff) with mixed ability. Setting is organized separately within the two main subjects Mathematics and English, and for a combined group of other academic subjects. The ideal is felt by some to be separate setting for every subject, but the small size of most departments fortunately makes this impossible. I believe there should be more subject groupings, which would permit greater adaptation within a setting system and lead to fruitful syllabus development.

In the English Department I have a reasonable degree of autonomy, and have taken advantage of it to broaden the ability ranges. At present there are two parallel top sets in English, and three parallel middle sets, determined annually by a standardized English test set over the whole ability range (see Appendix). The small bottom set, usually limited to about ten children, is outside the subject setting system, and its content is decided by the teachers involved, on the basis of an agreed list drawn up by the heads of Mathematics and English. I believe that such a modified form of streaming is helpful, especially in a period of adaptation to new teaching methods such as my department is experiencing.

In the fourth year pupils intending to take examinations are directed towards G.C.E. and C.S.E. classes. The choice is an invidious and silly one to have to make, but we do what we can to direct children to their greatest advantage. There is, of course, no restriction of choice arising from the set they may have been in during their first three years. The leavers are at present grouped into three mixed-ability classes for all subjects. A course for school-leavers, devised with their future jobs in mind, in association with local firms and departments, was planned by a group of teachers before I joined the school, and is being developed now. The English work is not yet integrated into the course in any significant way, but my syllabus has been planned with this in mind, and further consultation and syllabus planning for the non-examination course is taking place at present. My own impressions are that the course, good in its essentials, suffers from lack of adequate consultation amongst the staff implementing it. It could have too narrow a bias towards vocational training, and it may be that the specific contribution of the English Department will be to give a more liberal emphasis to the course.

English teaching in the school is in the hands of 9 teachers, 4 of them graduates (3 in English). A recent appointment amongst the others has been a drama specialist. English is now being planned along the lines of an experimental new syllabus, some extracts from which follow:

GENERAL PRINCIPLES

English differs from most other subjects, and especially other 'academic' subjects, on the school curriculum in a number of significant ways. It has been argued that it should not be called a subject at all, and there is much to be said for this. There is no clearly defined body of knowledge that a student must acquire; our pupils already have a working knowledge of vocabulary and syntax adequate to their immediate needs; and, in spite of what some teachers sincerely believe, there is no generally accepted grammar which can be committed to memory. What then is an English teacher trying to do? His aim is to extend the range within which the children can communicate and respond, and to enrich the means at their disposal of doing so. The two words 'communication' and 'response' will form the basis of all that follows here. In fulfilling this aim the English teacher will be concerned with the whole range of his pupils' experience, including all their school subjects. Conversely, every teacher who uses English as a means of communication must share the English teacher's concern for the medium of communication if he wishes to be fully effective in his work. In this sense the much abused cliché is still valid—'every teacher is a teacher of English'.

Children learn English first by imitation. From the very beginning their means of expression is closely involved with their whole personality. Through language they begin to gain control over the environment in which they find themselves. Through language—the language they hear around them—they first become aware of themselves as individuals, set apart from their environment. Any attack on a child's language forms, then, is an attack on the whole range of experiences and emotions that are bound up with them. Our job as English teachers necessitates first a sympathetic awareness of our pupils' environments. Unless we have some understanding of the sources of their present means of expression we have little hope of developing or refining it. For we cannot expect them to discard the whole framework of their means of communication and expression, however imperfect it may seem to us, in the interests of acquiring a 'standard' English, any more than we could expect them to deny the relationships brought about, or at any rate realized, by their grasp of language. Instead we must aim to increase their awareness of the potentialities of language by encouraging them to explore through it the worlds of external sensation, and of internal thought and feeling. Only when we have thus stimulated the flow of language, only when the children want, even need, to find new means of expression, can we begin to help them refine and extend it. From this emerges our first principle in English teaching: *Control of language can only grow out of a need for expression through language.*

In order to provide suitable stimuli we shall need to bear in mind three points: (1) Pupils must have a *context* within which their need for expression can find a natural place. Hence—(2) there must be a *theme* that can be clearly grasped by the pupils, that has enough intrinsic interest to catch and hold their attention, and that can provide enough variety of material to ensure a wide range of interest; and—(3) they must have an *audience* sufficiently clearly defined to focus the pupils' powers of communication, and sufficiently real for them to want to communicate with it.

A good working definition of 'correct English', linked with what has already been said, would be F. D. Flower's *language appropriate to the occasion of its use and effective in achieving the intentions of its author.* From this it follows that English which is correct in the context of, for instance, a B.B.C. news bulletin may be quite incorrect, i.e. inappropriate, and therefore failing of the desired effect, for a works' foreman giving orders to a construction gang. If we wish to improve our pupils' English we must first provide contexts within their experience that will make fuller demands on their language resources, and then help them towards finding the appropriate means of expression. The English syllabus is framed with this aim.

In the first section of the syllabus after this introduction I outline the environment within which teaching is carried on, pointing out that:

each class has to be assessed separately, each will make its own peculiar demands, and—while the aims are the same for all—each will arrive at fuller communication and response by different routes. Our job is to be sufficiently flexible, sensitive, sympathetic and honest to make this possible...

Worth-while communication will more often take place when the pupil feels himself to be an individual, and feels that his personality is recognized. There will be a class unity of course, but this may often be inimical to the most productive work in English. Children can often take refuge in 'the class' and see the teacher as pitted against it. It will be useful therefore to aim increasingly at work in discussion groups.

The section ends with an indication of the general pattern of work:

(i) as individuals working at their own pace with individual help from the teacher;

(ii) as members of discussion groups, preparing and discussing work, compiling reports and summaries, and presenting their work for criticism and evaluation to an audience (perhaps the rest of the class, perhaps the teacher, perhaps other parts of the school, parents or outside bodies);

(iii) as a class, usually consolidating work done in (i) and (ii), or being presented with new thematic material by the teacher.

The second section of the syllabus aims at defining the material on which English teaching will be based. In the first part reference is made to the inevitable connection between 'English' and all other school subjects, urging teachers to pursue such opportunities as arise of emphasizing the connection. Under the present rigid departmentalizing of subjects such opportunities are hard to find even when other subject teachers are sympathetic, as they often are, and this underlines the need for curriculum reform along the lines I suggested earlier. Section two continues with a clarification of what is involved in the thematic treatment of English:

Themes. A well-chosen theme related to what the teacher knows of his pupils and to their capabilities and maturity will provide both a wide variety of material and a unifying influence which will focus and make more real their use of English. The following scheme will provide the framework within which themes can be chosen and developed. Each of the ten branches of experience listed is obviously too wide to be used as a theme in itself, but every theme chosen should relate more closely to one or another of the ten, and if the teacher keeps them in mind they will help to ensure that no important part of human experience within the children's range is omitted. Wherever possible opportunities should be taken of linking themes with school subjects, and once the theme has been chosen many such opportunities will suggest themselves:

(i) personal health—physical, mental, spiritual;
(ii) possessions—toys, hobbies, pets, etc.;
(iii) families—relationships, parents' work and attitudes;
(iv) social groups outside family—Scouts, Guides, Youth Clubs, gangs, Church and Chapel;
(v) physical environment—homes, countryside or town, places of work, school, weather;
(vi) leisure—holidays, sport;
(vii) technology and the individual—e.g. transport, mass-production;
(viii) the mass-media—T.V., radio, newspapers and magazines;
(ix) world affairs—politics, underdeveloped countries, internationalism;
(x) the Arts.

Obviously some themes will relate to more than one of these—e.g. a theme of 'cars' could relate to (ii) and (vii) and perhaps others;

the list is offered as a general guide to help the teacher cover all important aspects of life as our pupils experience it.

It is envisaged that for the first two years themes will be chosen relating only to nos (i) to (vi). In the third year the field should be widened to include (vii), and from the fourth year onward all ten can be covered. There is likely to be less emphasis on (ii) and (iii) after the third year. It is stressed that English does not, like some other school subjects, 'go forward from the simple to the complex through a series of nice intermediate steps. Instead, it is to be viewed concentrically rather than vertically, the children covering the same kind of ground year by year, with progress shown only by their increasing ability to make sense of their environment, and by their power to express to others that awareness' (R. H. Poole and P. J. Shepherd, *Impact* (Heinemann, 1967), Teachers' Book, p. 3).

All successful English teaching on the lines proposed will depend very heavily on the relation built up between the teacher and his pupils. For this reason no specific themes can be laid down for use with particular forms. The teacher will choose his themes with his own and his class's special interests, aptitudes and limitations in mind, as well as with a weather eye open for opportunities available at the time (e.g. a current radio or T.V. series, a topical news-item, special local conditions). I envisage that a theme will normally cover four or five weeks' work, but its length will depend very much on its scope, and the interest it has aroused; an unsuccessful one—and there are bound to be failures, particularly at first—may be abandoned after a fortnight, while one that has given rise to plenty of ideas and enthusiasm may last a whole term. Teachers should be guided by (*a*) the response of the class; (*b*) the scope of the theme and its relation to the ten points given earlier; (*c*) the need to keep the pupils' minds and imaginations at full stretch, and to ensure continuity and development.

In the third section of the syllabus rather fuller suggestions are made for implementing the principles already outlined. I felt it would be helpful to give some guidance first over the proportions of available lesson-time to be devoted to different activities, especially bearing in mind those who only have a few

English lessons to teach. I shall explain later how we are modifying the suggestions in practice:

the following may be taken as a rough guide to the planning of English work along the lines suggested. For convenience a fortnight's lessons (i.e. 10 periods) are discussed; the same or similar proportions could well extend over the 5- or 6-week period of a theme.

(i) Whole class (3–4 lessons). One or two of these would be needed for presenting a new theme to the class, discussing its implications, and working out pupils' individual stints. At least one would be needed for introducing related literature—and occasionally *un*related literature—and giving guidance about where to find further material. Finally, one would probably be needed to focus attention on problems encountered as theme work progresses—including routine problems of writing (e.g. spelling, punctuation, paragraph control, standard practices in letters).

(ii) Discussion groups (3–4 lessons). These groups (*never* more than seven pupils) once established should normally have the same personnel for at least a term, and perhaps for the whole year. Discussions are generally more profitable as the members of the group become adjusted to one another. The class should be allowed to form themselves into groups, with discreet guidance from the teacher (e.g. if possible he should try to mix the sexes, at any rate in two or three of the groups). Each group will appoint a secretary or 'scribe', discuss the theme or aspects of it, and initiate work based on it. Useful guidance to the techniques of good discussion, and its difference from mere conversation, may be gained from tape-recording one group's discussion from time to time, playing back during one of the whole-class lessons. Each group in turn may be responsible for a display or form newspaper relating to the theme in hand, and for compiling the theme folder.

(iii) Individual work (2–3 lessons). Each pupil will have a special aspect or branch of the theme to explore. In addition *each will be following an independent project of his own*, probably lasting throughout the year and involving the compilation of a project note-book and/or folder. There will also need to be opportunities for pupils working on their own on particular exercises, and for individual reading-time. The teacher should be able to give some of his most valuable help during these lessons, aiming at seeing every pupil with his work in hand at least once in three or four weeks.

(iv) Drama (1–2 lessons). The separate drama syllabus will deal with this more fully. Opportunities for dramatic work, either improvised or scripted, will arise naturally out of the themes chosen and their associated reading-matter. The general approach must always be through acting rather than reading.

This is followed by separate sections on the three branches of English—speaking, writing and reading, considered as parts of a whole:

In general, the first- and second-year forms will need encouragement rather than criticism if they are to gain the necessary initial confidence in using English. While this means a certain emphasis on quantity and fluency it need not imply a lowering of standards. Self-criticism can only come when pupils find out for themselves that they are failing to communicate when they want to. We can then help them towards clarity and coherence because they themselves will understand the need for it. From the third year onward there will be increasing emphasis on the means whereby their language can be made more appropriate and effective.

Speaking. Pupils' speech-forms are already established when we first meet them. Our aims, in this order, are (*a*) to encourage the fullest use of them; (*b*) to show where they are inadequate; and (*c*) to extend and correct them, bearing in mind Flower's definition of 'correct English'. Pupils' standards in speech will reflect our own and those of our colleagues—if we are slovenly in expression and pronunciation we cannot expect them to be different. Drama will provide one of our chief means of developing an awareness of the potentialities of spoken English. Other opportunities for oral work are:

(i) in discussion groups, especially in reporting back to the class—undertaken by each group member in turn;

(ii) in following a line of enquiry in the course of theme work. This may necessitate interviewing, telephoning and questioning, both in and out of school;

(iii) in more formal talks to the class or to other audiences. These should always be given from notes (a strict word-limit is often a good idea) or 'off the cuff', not read...Opportunities should also be made for pupils to speak about their individual projects.

Writing. It will be helpful to adopt the following scheme for keeping track of English written work.

(i) Theme folders...One should be kept for each theme dealt with. It will be under the direct supervision of the teacher, but should be made available to any member of the group or class and kept in the classroom when it is complete. It will contain copies of letters sent, summaries of any visits, newspaper and other cuttings assembled in the course of theme-work, pictures and photographs, abstracts of talks given (either by class-members or outsiders), and individual contributions, e.g. poems, stories, reports.

(ii) English work-books. Each pupil will have one. These will be used for the following routine work:

(*a*) exercises in connection with any special problems or difficulties of expression—including handwriting exercises;

(*b*) notes for talks, discussions, etc.;

(*c*) individual written contributions to the theme (possibly duplicated in the theme folder);

(*d*) *at the back* (1) brief records in note-form of all themes tackled, with dates of starting and finishing [necessary for when pupils move from one class to another]; (2) a list of all books read (title, author, date, comment). A duplicated sheet is available from the librarian.

(iii) Individual project (book or folder). Pupils should be encouraged to provide their own, and to make it especially their own, perhaps by decorating the cover, or illustrating it. *On no account* should it contain any writing or marking by the teacher, unless the pupil specially requests it.

(iv) English writing in other subjects...Permission must be sought from time to time to see this, and to assess and mark the work from the point of view of English expression.

Reading. In the course of work on the lines suggested there will be many opportunities to incorporate reading that is appropriate and significant to the pupils. The concept of covering or 'doing' a certain minimum of 'classics' for their own sake rather than according to the children's ability to respond to them is I think a mistaken one. Instead we should aim at a three-fold approach.

(i) Reading in connection with themes. This need not be merely factual, though it will provide good opportunities of handling reference books. Wherever possible, school texts should be chosen that can be linked with the themes (e.g. the theme of 'city life' could make use of *A Kid for Two Farthings*; one connected with life in villages could incorporate a reading of *Silas Marner*). The list of available texts will allow for this kind of flexibility. Choices must be made in conjunction with other teachers of the same year-group.

(ii) Individual reading. This may be guided by theme-work, or by individual project work, but can be independent of either. Library book lists appropriate to age and ability will be provided by the librarian, and pupils should be encouraged to make the fullest use of school, town and county libraries. A check-list of all books read should be kept in English work-books, and teachers must try to encourage a minimum of three or four books read per term. The paperback book club 'Scoop' is very helpful both in encouraging private reading and in helping selection. Try to bring it frequently to the attention of the children. All English teachers will get copies of the lists as they come out.

(iii) Special enthusiasms. Teachers should from time to time find opportunities to transmit their own enthusiasms and to recommend personal choices, even when they lie outside theme-work altogether.

One of the two English homework periods should be set aside for reading, and some check should be made of pupils' use of this time. It is *not* recommended that a whole class should be set a reading stint of x pages in one homework, to be tested next day. This leads to the wrong kind of reading altogether, and will rapidly kill any interest there may have been in the book.

Reading for meaning. Apprehension rather than comprehension is the keynote to reading in the first two or three years. Only as the pupils gain maturity (roughly fourteen years and over) can they be expected to respond to an analytic study of reading-matter, or a detailed examination of a writer's method and vocabulary. Traditional comprehension exercises based on short passages out of context have a strictly limited value at any point, and are almost certainly harmful in the first two years at secondary school.

The question of books for English work is a difficult one. Most heads of English departments are familiar with the problems associated with text-books and readers—the miscellaneous collection inherited, the favoured 'course-books' hallowed by long, and one fears often insensitive, use with individual teachers, the dusty heaps of superannuated examination set works, etc. My inheritance at Newtown High School was complicated by remnants from the four different schools it superseded, listed in some half-dozen out-of-date inventories. What is more, in the general confusion of successive amalgamations teachers had acquired, in self-defence, squirrel-like habits of hoarding favourite texts. After rationalizing the existing situation I evolved a two-point system which is now gaining ground, and proving workable. First, I provide a complete list, revised annually, of all class sets available, grouped by years. This forms a basis for discussion and agreement between all the teachers of each year-group, in a series of meetings at the beginning of the year. The syllabus includes the following comment on the use of text-books:

The present school stock is under review, and will be progressively reduced and brought up to date. *It cannot be too strongly stressed that to work through a 'course-book' lesson by lesson is dangerously harmful to any real progress in English.* Text-books should be used as quarries for relevant material, not as courses. The annual book-list will give details of those available, and teachers must decide among themselves (*a*) which of them, if any, can be useful, and (*b*) whether to exchange them in the course of the year. *There is no obligation to use any text-books*, and the thematic method can be followed quite happily without one.

Secondly, I used an unexpected windfall from the authority to provide, with the co-operation of the Woodwork Department, book-boxes designed to hold up to fifty books, for use as portable libraries. The syllabus notes these as follows:

Book boxes will be provided for each form as stocks are built up. These boxes contain 8 titles each, in sets of 5, chosen with the age-range of the pupils in mind. One or two form members can take charge of the issue and return of books. By exchanging boxes termly or half-yearly 16 to 24 books can be made available. Teachers are asked to acquaint themselves with any books unknown to them, and to suggest additional titles, so as to incorporate the reading-matter into the syllabus more closely. It is planned to review and alter the content of the boxes frequently.

This scheme is proving popular in the department, and much of each year's requisition is devoted to small sets of reading-books for the boxes. A recent decision in a departmental meeting will now lead to the abandoning of class readers altogether from the third year on, in favour of book-box selections.

The main body of the syllabus concludes with some notes on that perennial English teacher's problem, marking:

Marking. However one approaches English work, it is bound to involve continual reading, assessment and encouragement of pupils' writing. Under present heavy teaching-loads in English, this imposes a formidable body of work on the teacher. Under the thematic scheme much, perhaps most, of this work should be done in the presence of the pupils. If marking is to be effective it must wherever possible be done while the work is fresh in the writer's mind. This suggests that to set a piece of written work to the entire class should be fairly rare, except for exercises dealing with specific difficulties that have arisen—which can probably be marked by the pupils themselves. I envisage groups and individuals handing in work for marking at different times, depending on the stages they have reached in their themes and individual projects, the teacher keeping a check of work seen so as to be sure of seeing all pupils' work at least every fortnight. In addition, as has already been said, teachers should seek opportunities of reading and marking work done in other subjects, especially those which depend heavily on written notes and essay-work. With the cooperation of the teachers concerned three or four pieces per pupil per term should be seen. Finally, the approach to English outlined here depends for its effectiveness on the relation built up between teacher and pupils, and therefore on qualities of the teacher as a person. A teacher distracted and overburdened with marking will be incapable of the demands of such an approach. In the last resort his efficiency as an English teacher is measured, not by the quantity and frequency of red marks in his pupils' exercise-books, but by the articulateness, fluency and maturity of the pupils themselves, and by their response to literature.

Marking should always be encouraging and helpful rather than merely fault-finding. A marking code has already been agreed upon in the English Department which helps to emphasize this. Each piece of work marked should be given three grades, each out of A–E, as follows:

(i) for liveliness, originality, efficient handling of material—what might be called the total *effectiveness* of the piece of writing in relation to its aims;

(ii) for the accuracy of the work, its success in using the accepted techniques (punctuation, paragraphing, reporting of speech, etc.) to get the writer's intentions across, and for conformity, within reason, with accepted spellings;

(iii) for the presentation of the work—clarity and gracefulness of hand-writing, setting out, and spacing.

These three grades are written at the end of the work thus: B/C/A, and may be further modified by adding + or – after the grade. In assessing work, teachers should try to measure the pupil's achievement and effort in terms of his own ability rather than by grading him in a class-merit order.

In order to help teachers in their approach to this kind of work, I included a supplement to the syllabus:

FOUR GUIDE-LINES FOR ENGLISH TEACHERS

I. An English teacher should be actively involved in teaching the subject for the whole of every English lesson, and for an unspecified number of hours per week outside lesson-time, in the proportion of about two to five (i.e. 5 periods of teaching necessitating 2 periods of marking and preparation).

Note. The way this involvement shows itself will depend on the type of lesson, e.g. (*a*) *group work*—the teacher is spending time with each group in turn, joining in the discussion, suggesting new lines of approach, listening to points made, controlling the distribution of written work connected with the group theme; (*b*) *individual projects*—the teacher is checking pupils' work individually, going over mechanical errors, suggesting new ways of tackling the topic, referring the pupils to books, magazines, and other sources of material; (*c*) *class teaching*—the teacher deals with a specific English skill, or isolates a particular point that has arisen in the course of theme and project work. She sets exercises on such work, and controls the marking of them, whether it is done by her or by the pupils themselves. The teacher may also introduce new material for theme or project work, or follow up some other branch of English that can best be dealt with in a class lesson, such as debate, talks by pupils, poetry, etc.

II. The children (and their parents) should realize always that their work, whether oral or written, is the active and continual concern of their English teacher, so that at no time can they feel that the way they write or speak does not matter.

Note. Traditionally this principle has been put into practice by the regular marking of written work, especially compositions. Our more flexible and realistic approach to English studies does not alter the principle. Teachers should ensure that they have seen every pupil's written work *at least once a fortnight*, and the pupils should know this, and should be aware of the standard they have reached in each piece of work as it is done. In English work-books this will be evident from the teacher's written assessment using three grades, each out of A–E, for ideas and originality, mechanical correctness, and presentation; in individual projects there will normally be no marks visible, but the teacher will have a record of the work as a result of his regular supervision of it, and the pupil should know what he is achieving week by week in this, as in any other English work. In group-work each pupil may be contributing to a group folder, but often such work will also appear in the work-books.

III. The teacher should satisfy himself that the pupil's reading is both wide-ranging and progressive. Pupils will look to him for guidance, and should develop their standards of what constitutes worth-while reading through their English work in school.

Note. The established methods of book-box selections, library lists, and occasional class-texts will all help. If the teacher feels that time is needed for silent reading in English lessons, the reading thus done should be of recognized worth. At no time should it be possible for pupils to spend English class time reading or skimming through meretricious material. During silent reading sessions the teacher will normally be involved either in actively ensuring that these standards are maintained, or in marking and assessing other English work done by that class.

IV. The aim should be kept clearly in mind that every piece of work—theme, project, play, talk, debate—needs to be completed. To leave work unfinished or to prevent its completion seriously impairs its value to the children. They should be able to experience frequently in their English the satisfaction of completing a piece of work. This will be to them the clearest evidence they can get of progress in the subject.

Note. This basic principle is difficult to apply systematically to project work. Children can rarely see the end of a project when they start on it, and will often choose far too wide and ambitious a topic. Teachers will need to limit the scope of such projects so that they can be completed in a reasonable time. There are probably very few pupils who can sustain their interest in one project for more than a term, and most should aim at completing one in a shorter period.

IMPLEMENTING THE SYLLABUS

On the whole, the syllabus has been accepted by the English teachers, and we are now meeting termly to discuss the practical problems involved in working it. One that has repeatedly cropped up, and will have to be tackled systematically, is the need for collections of materials for theme-work. It is good to see that publishers are alive to the needs of this kind of work, and are slowly moving towards the idea that an English course-book is not necessarily the only way of supplementing the staple diet of 'readers', poetry and plays. We have already started to make use of Michael Marland's *Pictures for Writing* (Blackie, 1966), the new Longmans poetry series in sets of booklets grouped according to themes—a promising venture —and Geoffrey Summerfield's Penguin anthologies of poetry and pictures, *Voices*. I am at present working on a projected series of 'English theme kits', which will aim at providing material relating to particular themes in a variety of media. The proliferation of course-books still continues however, and it would be interesting to know how far this is a genuine attempt to meet a demand, and how far it stems from the publishers' pursuit of an easy market. It is depressing to think that heads of English departments are still placing bulk orders for such books, and thus committing their schools and their English staffs for six or seven years ahead. Even the best of English course-books cannot really stand up to such rigid acceptance with all that it implies of lesson-by-lesson plodding through. At Newtown we are hoping to cater for our needs partly by using the book-box scheme, devoting a box to a single theme, the eight choices all relating to it. For the rest we are dependent on our own resourcefulness in utilizing what is to hand—pupils' own materials and photographs, local stimuli of every kind, the press, radio and television.

A second difficulty concerns the mechanics of theme and project work. (For the sake of clarity we use the term 'theme' for work done with groups or classes, and 'project' for work done individually.) Teachers have found it difficult to maintain pupils' interest in, and to keep track of, both theme and project work at the same time. At an English meeting we discussed the possibility of concentrating on theme-work in one term and project work in the next, and this may be a workable solution.

Another practical problem is that of organizing group-work in the inadequate space of a classroom. With five or six discussion groups the noise level is bound to rise, and this tends to reduce the value and continuity of discussions. The long-term answer is purpose-built accommodation, as it is for drama; the standard classroom of about 480 square feet is too small for a class of thirty to do group-work comfortably. At least 600 square feet of floor space is needed, with suitably damped wall and ceiling surfaces to reduce resonance. Meanwhile we resort to various makeshifts, such as sending one group into a neighbouring room, or even a cloakroom space, allowing groups to meet two or three at a time while the rest of the class read or work on their own, and so on. In conjunction with the Craft Department at Newtown I have planned and we have constructed a sound-muffled discussion booth, which is effective for groups of six or seven. Messrs F. Llewellyn & Company Ltd, of Liverpool, are developing the invention, and have already produced prototypes for trial purposes, so they could be in production within a year or so. Until purpose-built English teaching rooms become general these portable booths may well prove invaluable.

These are immediate and practical problems, and we can tackle them empirically as they arise. But this concept of English teaching raises more fundamental problems that relate to our whole educational structure. In the first place it calls in question the present pattern of rigidly departmentalized 'subjects' in secondary schools, and indeed the whole concept of specialization on which it is based. This concept, bolstered by the pay structure, has in many ways served us well in the grammar schools, where it has encouraged high standards within the various specialist disciplines, even though the element of competition between them has not always been educationally sound—and all grammar-school teachers know how much pressure can be placed on fourth and fifth formers by unscrupulous specialists anxious to snaffle the best academic material for their sixth form.

I do not think we can accept this kind of attitude with any complacency in the comprehensive schools. Instead we should be pressing for a radical re-shaping of the curriculum, along lines that are already being examined in some research project, so as to encourage cooperation between allied subject-disciplines. At present many teachers who want to do this find themselves shackled by a rigid time-table planned exclusively along subject lines; this in turn encourages a narrow conformism and some mental indolence in both teachers and taught.

At Newtown I have felt this increasingly. The time-table is planned in 8 teaching periods per day (5 and 3), and again and again one hears staff grumbling that the lesson—frequently no more than thirty minutes allowing for movement between periods—has been too short. The continual demands for variety of 'options' (and we are now familiar with the curious spectacle of neighbouring grammar and comprehensive schools window-dressing with a wide range regardless of its real educational value) seem to leave no alternative. Yet how can we really justify such arbitrary fragmentation of the teaching day, especially with less able pupils? One only has to step into a classroom with, let us say, second-year set six children for the last period of the afternoon to see the futility of it. Moreover even the best teacher—perhaps he especially—finds it well-nigh impossible to give of his best when he is expected to make seven or eight re-adjustments to different classes in a single day, and to respond adequately, in consequence, to upwards of 200 different personalities. Such a system actively encourages dull and stereotyped teaching methods; I often find myself resorting to them in sheer self-defence.

Ironically the time-table makers in schools are less aware of this trend than other staff because they have shed much of their teaching load in the interests of administration. Clearly the only long-term answer will be to organize the teaching day in much longer 'blocks'—say three a day—and to group the subjects into their related disciplines under such headings as 'humanities', 'social studies', 'language', 'physical science', or even along lines such as those suggested by Raymond Williams in *The Long Revolution* (Penguin Books, 1965, Part II, chapters I, IV). Within such a structure, theme and project work would find its fullest justification, and we could begin to correct the myopia induced by our present over-specialization. The much debated problems of setting/streaming would also, I believe, prove less imponderable; as teachers themselves began to explore the relationships between allied subjects instead of merely pursuing their own specialisms they would more readily adapt their methods to a wider ability range. In a day of normal social and business intercourse we take it for granted that we should adapt readily and promptly to many different social and intellectual levels. Is there any valid reason for refusing to do so in the classroom?

At Newtown I have discussed informally this question of time-tabling for longer teaching periods with the head of Mathematics, and we have drawn up a scheme for a fifty-period fortnight (five hours per day) which we believe would ease a number of time-tabling problems relating to practical subjects—especially Nuffield science—as well as being more realistically related to the actual teaching situation than the present frantic working day. The chief opposition to the scheme seems likely to come from language teachers, who prefer the principle of 'little and often', but it should not be impossible to achieve some sort of compromise. There are certainly schools where this pattern is already operating successfully.

Some of these observations point to methods already generally accepted in the primary schools, and I believe we need urgently to pursue every opportunity of meeting primary-school teachers and discussing with them educational methods. The new teachers' centres will help here, together with organizations like the National Association for the Teaching of English, but we ought also to expect local departments and colleges of education to give a lead in promoting and planning such fruitful dialogue. At Newtown our nearest department of education is at Aberystwyth, but so far I have looked in vain for any such liaison, in spite of the fact that we accept students regularly for teacher-training. Successive English students seem to have no idea we are working along untraditional lines—indeed they seem not to know that such ideas are current in English teaching today—and are totally unprepared for any teaching that involves relinquishing 'the disappearing dais'. I hope this is untypical, for we shall need all the cooperation and guidance we can get if we are to develop the new methods.

In connection with this I believe that the whole question of the secondment of practising teachers needs to be aired. Teachers need the stimulus of frequent contact with educational theory and research just as lecturers in colleges and departments of education need the stimulus of frequent practice in school-teaching. Is it too much to hope for York University's system of exchanges to become the normal pattern? One cannot help viewing with some misgiving the recent trend towards regarding training-college posts as a haven for timid grammar-school teachers faced with comprehensivization. Moreover, less progressive local education authorities can at present veto automatically any requests for secondment by practising teachers. Surely there is a need here for legislation to ensure that teachers can claim as of right a certain minimum period—say a term in five years—for secondment to research or refresher courses.

On the whole the secondary educational environment at Newtown is a good one. Comprehensive education is generally accepted as the rational solution in a thinly populated area, and the traditional Welsh respect for education is still apparent in the attitudes of parents and children. Wales is very productive of teachers—one might call them the Principality's chief 'export'—which leads to the preponderance of Welsh staff in the school which I noted earlier. I think such a bias in an increasingly self-conscious nation has its disadvantages, leading to a certain insularity that is enhanced in Newtown by the physical distances from any urban centre. In the organization of English work I have been given a free hand and have had a high degree of cooperation and support from the headmaster. The chief difficulties encountered in the work I have outlined here have arisen from the fact that one is to some extent swimming against the current, and making demands on pupils which they find it hard to adapt to when for the rest of their lessons they are expected to conform along traditional lines. I suspect that 'English', so long as it remains one specialist subject amongst others, will always seem radical in this way. If by being so it is stimulating teachers and pupils into re-assessing their contribution to school as a truly educational environment it is performing a valuable service.

APPENDIX

I. SOME PROPOSALS FOR GENERAL STUDIES IN THE SIXTH FORM AT NEWTOWN HIGH SCHOOL

It is suggested that the General Studies course be organized on a team teaching basis, involving between eight and twelve teachers depending on the size of the sixth forms (see Note 3 below). The course could be planned as a whole by the teachers involved, so as to draw attention to the wider implications of the different specialisms in a secondary school and the common aims of the education provided through them. The team of teachers should therefore be as fully representative as possible of the different academic and other disciplines. Each teacher would be expected to prepare and deliver one or two lectures to the rest, staff and sixth-formers, during the year; the subject matter would be agreed upon beforehand by the whole staff team. The session might also include one or two visiting speakers.

Assuming that initially one double lesson were devoted to the scheme (i.e. approximately 20 staff teaching periods per week), the course might be organized in fortnightly sections, as follows:

First double lesson	(*a*)	*1 hour.* Lecture to all sixth forms and staff involved in scheme.
	(*b*)	*approx. 30 mins.* Discussion groups with individual teachers (including the setting of written work).
Second double lesson	(*a*)	*approx. 30 mins.* Discussion groups. Return of written work, further discussion leading to the formulation of questions and comments for (*b*).
	(*b*)	*1 hour.* Forum—teachers involved form panel to deal with questions and comments, chaired by previous week's speaker.

Notes. (1) Time-table:

(*a*) The sixth-form lessons needed would have to be put on the time-table *before* any specialist subjects, so as not to exclude any sixth-former; the success of the scheme would depend on 100 percent sixth-form attendance.

(*b*) It would be helpful to time-table the double period either immediately before or immediately after the dinner break, so as to extend the time available if necessary.

(*c*) A big room, preferably the hall, would be needed, and probably three or four small rooms as well. The hall could house at least four of the discussion groups. All the rooms should be available for the whole double period, so as to avoid restricting speakers or discussion groups.

(2) Lectures and lecture-notes: each teacher would be called upon to deliver only one or two lectures during the year. It would be helpful if the lectures could provide brief notes in advance, including explanations of any specialized or technical terms, to the other teachers in the group. These could include suggested topics for further discussion and for written work.

(3) Discussion groups: the maximum number in a group for worth-while discussion is 8 pupils, and the ideal is probably 5 or 6. Thus a sixth form of 70 to 80 would need 10 teachers. The composition of the groups should be planned so as to include as wide a range as possible, and in particular so as to include both science and arts pupils.

(4) Written work: a short piece of written work could be set each fortnight, and this need not impose too great a burden either on pupils or on teachers. The necessity for pupils to organize their ideas in writing should help to avoid superficiality, and lead to more cogent and profitable discussions.

(5) Examinations: such a course does not need the justification of an external examination, although some examining boards do in fact set General Studies papers at O- and A-levels and the possibility of entering pupils might be discussed further. Similarly an internal school examination might be set, if teachers felt it would be useful.

These proposals were accepted more or less on the lines laid down here. In 1968–9 we were able to have only five teachers, representing the following subject disciplines: English, Geography, Mathematics, Modern Languages, Music. The year's work was devised within the framework of two general themes, 'communication' and 'democracy'. For the first we had one outside speaker in addition to the five team members; in the second theme we included a film—*The Best Man*—on 'democratic' election procedure in the U.S.A., and a visit from a senior executive of the Mid-Wales New Town Development Corporation. The latter was especially interesting in view of the plans for the development of Newtown, published shortly before the visit.

For the four or five weeks in the summer term when the upper sixth were involved in external examinations, we placed the initiative in the hands of the lower sixth. Activities included debates, a session of plays and music, and a visit to Ludlow, where pupils had a choice between watching the open-air production of *Romeo and Juliet* in the castle and exploring this ancient town and preparing a report on aspects that interested them, to be presented orally in a subsequent General Studies session at school.

The first team of teachers involved found the course both stimulating and wearing. We found it a considerable initial struggle in an examination-orientated sixth form to convince pupils that General Studies matter, that the further education to which they aspired would (or should) set a high premium on the adventurousness of mind demanded by such a course. The second problem, foreseen but not overcome, was that the discussion groups—normally 12–14—were too large for full involvement. In 1969–70 we have a team of 6: ideally there should be at least 8 to 75 pupils. My own feeling is that a course of this kind should be the 'core' of non-specialist sixth-form studies, and should be supplemented by a range of options from which pupils may choose in such a way that their choices complement rather than duplicate their specialisms.

II. THE STANDARDIZED TESTS (SEE p. 47)

These have been adapted from tests devised by the head of the English Department at Colne Valley High School, Yorkshire, and cover what might be called the more formal English skills. We supplement them by a test of continuous writing, for which we aim at a wide variety of choice, and attempt standardization of marks by multiple impression marking. The English sets for the following year are determined by combining the marks for both examinations, then subjecting the results to careful scrutiny and revision in a series of meetings by the English teachers for each year. I think we still have much to learn in this procedure, but it does ensure fairness, and mistakes can be quickly rectified by moving individuals from one English set to another. In any case the relatively wide ability range within English sets reduces any harmful effects there may be from misplacing. It seems likely that we may replace our own tests by the more scientific *Bristol Achievement Tests* (Nelson) in the near future.

III. C.S.E. MODE 3

In 1966 I invited English teachers from all six secondary schools in Montgomeryshire to a meeting to discuss the possibility of a Mode 3 C.S.E. syllabus for the county. There was little or no enthusiasm for such a plan, the teachers seeming unduly timid of relying on their own assessments of their pupils, so we have decided to go ahead independently at Newtown. We have now planned C.S.E. work on the lines of the following syllabus, which has been accepted by the Welsh Joint Education Committee. The first candidates were presented in 1970.

SYLLABUS FOR THE CERTIFICATE IN SECONDARY EDUCATION, MODE 3

The English Department is now planning English teaching along lines laid down in a new syllabus. While allowing for considerable variation between the methods adopted by individual teachers the syllabus on the whole aims at developing English ability and skills through the pursuit of themes and projects, both in groups and individually. We feel that the C.S.E. should reflect this approach, and as far as possible should be based on the work done during the fourth and fifth years at school. We feel also that substantially the same method of examining could be used in place of the G.C.E. Ordinary Level English language paper, and would provide a more reliable measurement of pupils' ability in English.

Assessment for the C.S.E. should be made within the following categories; the proportions suggested provide in our view a realistic indication of the relative importance for C.S.E. pupils of their needs in English:

I.	Oral and aural English	40 percent
II.	Written English	40 percent
III.	Reading	20 percent

I. Oral and aural English. The pupils' control over the spoken word will be their most important asset when they leave school. It is proposed to measure this in *four ways*, each accounting for 10 percent of the total marks which will determine the C.S.E. grade.

(i) Teacher's general assessment on ability to communicate effectively to and with others, based on continuous teaching and assessment from the beginning of the fourth year.

(ii) Ability in group discussion—both as discussion leader and as an active participant. This should again be assessed over the two years, but assessments will be 'moderated' by an outside examiner for purposes of standardization.*

(iii) Individual talk (on topic of own choice, preferably in connection with topic chosen for II. ii—see below) to a suitable audience—probably the remaining C.S.E. candidates. This too will be externally moderated.*

(iv) Ability in listening, observing and reporting, and in acting on specific instructions. In this section parts (*a*) and (*b*) could be carried out in the language laboratory, the tapes being subsequently available for external moderation.

- (*a*) short passage(s) read to the candidates, followed by questions requiring oral answers [the passage(s) being non-imaginative];
- (*b*) a film-strip, short film, or illustration(s) requiring some interpretation, followed by a spoken report by the candidate;
- (*c*) simple instructions, possibly over the telephone, on which candidates have to act. They are assessed as to their accuracy in carrying them out.

II. Written English. It is felt that the stress often laid on written examination papers does not provide the clearest indication of candidates' powers of written expression. We therefore propose to measure writing ability in *four ways*, each again accounting for 10 percent of the total marks:

(i) Teacher's assessment based on course work in English *and* in other subjects requiring powers of expression in writing. It is proposed that at least *two* pieces of written work per term should be done from notes under supervision in the classroom, and submitted for moderation as evidence supporting the teacher's assessment.

The type of work will depend on themes and projects in hand, but should include both imaginative and non-imaginative uses of language.

(ii) Individual project. This should be on a topic of the pupil's choice, and will normally be in a loose-leaf folder or folio. Stress is laid on the fact that these will remain the property of the pupils themselves, and will contain no teacher's corrections. They should be started in the fourth year and submitted on completion during the spring term in the fifth year. The project should contain evidence of (*a*) powers of continuous writing, and of the organization of a mass of material; (*b*) ability to handle standard works of reference.

(iii) A written paper (2 to 2½ hours) to test ability in English skills such as letter-writing, preparation of notes, messages and instructions. A set of dictionaries will be provided for this part of the examination, and ability to glean specific information from the dictionary will be tested.†

(iv) A piece of imaginative writing, prose or verse, to be prepared and submitted within a period of 7 to 14 days during the summer term in the fifth year. A list of subjects will be given covering as wide a range as possible within the candidate's imaginative grasp, and taking into account any special fields of experience relating to the locality.†

III. Reading. The results of wide and discriminating reading such as our syllabus recommends and encourages will be seen in the candidate's control over both spoken and written English. We do not believe in the efficacy of a separate Literature paper to stimulate the right kind of reading. We propose therefore that candidates' reading should be assessed in two parts, accounting respectively for 12 percent and 8 percent of the total marks, as follows:

(i) Library lists are provided throughout the school course. From these, and other books read during the English course, the candidates will be asked to submit a list of recent reading. The list must contain *at least eight books*, plus a poetry anthology chosen from those made available to them. Not more than *two* of the books may be class readers [this proviso will be unnecessary when the book-box scheme is fully in operation, because there will be no class readers in fourth- and fifth-year classes], and the list must contain at least three fictional and at least three non-fictional books. Candidates must be prepared to discuss the books in their list with the teacher, and sample discussions could be taped for external moderation.†

(ii) Reading aloud to an audience of short suitable passages of prose and/or verse from books in their own list. Candidates should be given the passages in time to prepare them, and will be assessed primarily for their understanding of the text.

Notes. (1) It will be noticed that no reference is made to drama. Much of the drama done in school will bear fruit in the pupils' command of spoken English. A separate drama syllabus is under preparation, and we propose in due course to submit a separate C.S.E. syllabus in drama based on the school syllabus.

(2) It is understood that the principle has been established, where Mode 3 already operates, of teachers receiving remuneration for any extra work involved in setting and marking the examination over and above normal teaching. While much of this syllabus arises directly out of the day-to-day teaching, it will be appreciated that certain parts, notably I. iv (replaying of tapes for assessment) and II. ii and iv, will demand such extra work.

* We have included with the syllabus detailed suggestions for moderating the kind of oral testing we consider desirable, and these have been amplified in response to queries from the examining board.

† A specimen paper and list of subjects for imaginative writing (II. iii and iv), and specimens of the library lists are included with the syllabus.

Guide-lines for unstreamed English at Settle High School

GRAHAM WHITE

Settle High School is a four-form entry comprehensive school of 600 pupils—338 girls and 262 boys; with 58 pupils in the sixth form. It was originally a one-form entry girls' grammar school and in 1958 it became a mixed comprehensive for children from eleven to eighteen years of age. The school is situated on the banks of the River Ribble in an attractive rural area of the West Riding of Yorkshire, with Settle as a small market town (population, 2,300) at the centre of an extensive and entirely rural catchment area of some 240 square miles.

The admission and exclusion procedure is anomalous and complicated: selection operates in eight parts of the area for either a direct grant grammar school, secondary modern schools, a public school, and the comprehensive school; which leaves approximately the remaining one-half of the area with an unselected entry into the comprehensive school. Although the school is 'creamed' by the local public school, which has endowed scholarships for local boys, and by the more distant maintained grammar school, we, thanks to the dubious merits of the Thorne scheme which has now displaced the 11+ in the area, 'cream off' other parts of the area so that the school does have a full range of ability; and although most of the children come from farming families, the intake represents pretty well the social content of the area.

The implications of this selection procedure for the school are far-reaching and whether or not the imbalance in the ratio of girls to boys in the school is due entirely to a fact of population, the truth is that abolition of selection envisaged for the area and the addition of those local boys who at present go by scholarship to the local public school would do much for the comprehensive school, whilst those primary schools now involved in selection ought only to benefit from a new-found freedom in their teaching.

The many, scattered, small primary schools with differences of aims and approaches to the teaching of English make liaison between schools difficult, whilst for the many children coming from scattered villages and isolated farm-houses (the smallest village has a population of 14, and there are some dozen other villages with a population of less than 60) the common problem for young children of making new friendships in a 'big' school is even more accentuated here, and can continue over a long time. Travelling to school can mean for some a morning walk across moors in all kinds of weather to catch a school bus for a one-hour journey to school for 8.30 a.m.; and then, at 3.20 p.m., a quick exit from school to catch what for some is the only available transport home. For some children the school day may well be the only opportunity for sustained social contact with other children of their own age. Even though there are many cases of pupils prepared to cycle some ten miles home after a meeting of an orchestral or discussion group held after school hours, after-school activities have to work hard to flourish and so as much opportunity as possible is given for activities of all kinds to take place inside and outside school during lunch-time breaks: music-making, reading, dances, sport, Youth Club activities and in an annexe of the school, drama, chess, talks, fund-raising.

Pupils suffer from a lack of cultural amenities in the area: there are few, if any, bookshops, cinemas, and theatres. The small village communities are very largely self-reliant with a community life and Church-based activities that involve the very young children and the older inhabitants but do not seem able to accommodate those teenagers who are not drawn into the flourishing Young Farmers' Clubs. The school has to try to serve these needs: it is used as a Youth Club and further education centre, and long-distance travelling to theatres and paperback book sales have become commonplace.

SCHOOL ORGANIZATION

Until 1965, the children were streamed in all subjects other than English and the so-called non-academic subjects in which they were taught in house-groups of mixed ability. The grading of the pupils was based on reports from the primary schools which were varied in standard since about half of the children come from one-, two-, or three-teacher schools, some having a full register of only twelve pupils, a few even smaller. Comparing standards for some 120 completely unknown children is difficult, if not impossible, and also perhaps unnecessary and time-wasting; many teachers had to spend a great deal of time operating their own do-it-yourself 11+ examination for the first year's intake.

At the beginning of the summer term in 1965, the headmaster and staff investigated the possibilities of extending the teaching in mixed-ability classes. Now (1968) all classes in the first year are unstreamed in all subjects, and so, too, in the second year, except for French where there are three sets. In the third year there are two sets in French, four sets in the separate sciences of Physics, Biology and Chemistry, two sets and two unstreamed classes in Mathematics, all other classes being unstreamed. In the fourth year pupils proceed to make a subject choice when in addition to English, Mathematics, two Craft subjects, Religious and Physical Education, they can choose in consultation with staff and parents five other subjects from twenty-two at G.C.E. and C.S.E. levels as part of a two-year course.

Those who in the fourth year intend to leave at fifteen, or who are not able to enter the courses made up of the choices above, go into one of two forms where English, Mathematics, General Studies, Rural Studies, Science, Music and Crafts are taken. They also have a projects afternoon with a choice from Music (choir-singing, music-making, instrumental work, guitar classes), Domestic Science and Cookery, Woodwork, Metalwork, Drama, Film-making, Photography, Science, and Rural Studies.

In the fifth year the pupils take G.C.E. O-level and the C.S.E. at the end of the two-year course begun in the fourth year. There is a one-year commercial course in the sixth form for those who have taken some external examinations in the fifth year and who want an introduction to Commerce, Shorthand, Typewriting, Bookkeeping and Accounts. The sixth form take A-level G.C.E. courses in eleven subjects.

The early mistakes and problems that occurred in the teaching of English to unstreamed classes were caused perhaps by a combination of over-buoyant enthusiasm and lack of organized preparation; yet it might be said that the paradox holds good that if these had not been present then the impetus for unstreaming might not have got under way when it did. It is clear now that the first steps in unstreaming in English, a single lesson each week in the first year, proved nothing; when a second-year form was being taught in unstreamed classes in English only, the pupils quite noticeably carried over habits and attitudes into their English lessons from the other streamed classes; and moreover the then unstreamed groups were imbalanced in the sense that there were in some of the forms as many as six who needed remedial work and three or four of the very brightest pupils of that year. Since then, when mixed-ability classes were extended almost fully, attempts were made to try to ensure that the four house-groups in which the pupils were taught were more proportionately balanced, and that no marked weighting occurred in numbers of pupils of either high or low ability.

The English Department has three full-time specialists, two who, in addition to teaching English, have other responsibilities, and a teacher in charge of remedial work for a small number of seriously backward children who are withdrawn from some lessons for special help. We ensure that these children spend at least half their time in their house-group for English lessons so that they are not siphoned off as a group from the general school as a whole or their house-group in particular. These pupils accommodate themselves easily and frequently very forcibly in drama lessons or lessons given over to discussion, and in most cases it is not very long before they are in their house-group on a full-time basis.

ENGLISH: THEMES AND TOPICS

We regard the subject 'English' as so closely concerned with an individual's growth that language is co-extensive with life itself. In the classroom, pupils and teachers should meet to share everyday experiences of encounters with life; the pupils should learn how to order and shape their experiences through the use of language. The change from the friendly, intimate, pupil-oriented teaching of the primary schools to the more aloof, impersonal, subject-oriented teaching that still characterizes the secondary school is something we aim to combat in our teaching of English—at least in the first three years.

On entering the secondary school, many pupils still like using words, playing with words, telling stories, swapping tales—they are so incorrigibly interested in themselves, in others, in their world, that the capacity for delight that children bring to school in their first year must be tapped and built upon. The teacher has only to listen, to tactfully allow them to give expression to their interests, obsessions, curiosities, and the classes will generate their own 'subject material' that the teacher can develop and extend. The relationship between the teacher and his pupils, the spirit of the classroom, becomes the first essential and it might well be more important than any material he has brought into the class, although the right poem or short story may well help to establish the relationship.

The teacher needs to adopt, at first, the role of the listener, forcing the class to communicate with one another as much as with himself, and demonstrate a belief that their thoughts and opinions and feelings are worth attention so that they can be allowed to emerge as individual persons rather than parts of an amorphous class. Once freed to talk about matters *they* feel are important, with the teacher showing his willingness and interest in listening, the class in turn will develop an attitude where they will be ready to be interested in the concerns of the teacher. This demands an imaginative sympathy, with the teacher dropping his public mask and showing his private face more, for there will be matters raised that are often not complimentary to the teacher himself, embarrassing questions, which will usually be the real concerns of growing people. The teacher will find himself involved in educating in the pupils an awareness of their own and other people's feelings, wants and interests, of getting them to identify feelings of shame, anxiety, love, hate; the more carefully they observe other people and try to record this observation, the more controlled will be their use of language.

Much of this will arise from the teaching of an unstreamed class, and this requires the selection of material for study which will be of common interest and worth to all the class, something which they can all have the opportunity of talking about, acting or improvising on, and writing about. In the same way, too, a homework assignment or written task should arise naturally from the matter of the lesson of that day, and should be within the range of all abilities. It also should be capable of unlimited extension so that the brightest pupil, on the one hand, can exercise his or her skill and imagination fully, and the slowest learner, on the other hand, does not feel the task beyond his or her interest and capability.

This is a task that the teaching of unstreamed classes imposes upon us and it is a problem of reconciling the claims of equality with those of excellence. In practice there is no real reason why it cannot be realized. Just as in the English lessons we aim at work that comes close to being an enjoyable extension of the pupils' own interests, so, in the literature we introduce, we look for those archetypal situations concerned with parents, home and school, with which the pupils are likely to be preoccupied; myth, legend and fairy-tale; fear, love, anger, fantasy and curiosity; the 'secret places' of which David Holbrook writes: the exploring of problems and the opportunity of giving expression to the vigour and zest for life that young people have.

There is, too, the advantage of variety which an unstreamed class of pupils can offer, since the children will come from different backgrounds with varying interests. Lessons can become livelier because of the diverse experience brought to the work in hand—'less able' pupils can often write, improvise, and talk with more imagination and vigour than children from a more protective, self-concerned home when, for instance, the work is an improvised drama on a family situation, or a recreation of the adventurous, exuberant daring of childhood play as explored in, for example, 'Through the Tunnel' by Doris Lessing, Bill Naughton's short stories, or the *Lore and Language of Schoolchildren* by the Opies. The pupils are easily interested in what might seem to be superficial things like making dams, trolleys, caves, dens, woods, the street, imaginary friends, flying, or swimming underwater, and if fetters are not placed upon the imagination then such things can become charged with the significance that G. M. Hopkins's 'inscape' writing produces in his journal entries:

At the end of the month hard frosts. Wonderful downpour of leaf: when the morning sun began to melt the frost they fell at one touch and in a few minutes a whole tree was flung of them; they lay masking and papering the ground at the foot. Then the tree seems to be looking down on its cast self as blue sky on snow after a long fall, its losing, its doing.

The rural life, the immediate environment of the school, informs the attitudes and outlooks of the pupils and provides an excellent opportunity for observing at first hand the farm activities of haymaking, milking, farm sales and lambing. There are the limestone scars and pavements of clints and grykes on the fells, the caves, pot-holes, quarries, skulls, bones and fossils littering the moors which the pupils can observe closely, exercising their five senses. They can 'capture' what they observe, and see metaphors and emblems of time all about them. There is the local village graveyard, the rivers, waterfalls, the poultry and sheep in the Rural Studies Department of the school, the 'found objects' to look at, talk about, write about. The poetry of John Clare, Edward Thomas, R. S. Thomas, Ted Hughes, William Dunlop, Seamus Heaney, Sylvia Plath's 'Wuthering Heights' and the writing of Liam O'Flaherty, Flora Thompson, Adrian Bell, Laurie Lee, Fred Kitchen and many others on country matters is ready to hand for looking at familiar things in a new way.

The pupils are not encouraged to pay too much attention to the 'striking phrase' if it inhibits them from speaking or writing honestly and truthfully, with their own words. Rather the aim is to use stories, poems, songs, riddles, pictures, gramophone records, walks to stimulate and give access to the use of words to recreate experience and open up the imagination. The basic aim is not so much to teach how to write, but how to create a need to write, and then to try to say what is really meant and felt. The elimination of mistakes in punctuation, expression, spelling, and handwriting will be motivated and overcome, by degrees, by the realization of the need to share experience and enjoyment. The subject matter is as important as its expression, content and form are interdependent, and the pupil learns to use language more effectively by active participation and involved interest so that, in Seamus Heaney's words, at first

They trip
To fall into themselves unknowingly.

The choice of literature for use in the classroom will be for its common interest and worth to a class of mixed ability. The literature will have to throw light on an aspect of the pupils' lives so that they and the teacher can apply the relevance and truth of the literature to illuminate the pupils' intellectual and emotional experience, extend their range of understanding, and widen their experience of the resources of language. The choice, too, can depend on the relationship between a class and a teacher, and it is the policy of the department that there should be, wherever possible, a continuity of class and teacher from the first year through the school to the fourth year. The relationship developed from the early days will be more likely to increase the range of material that a teacher can introduce to his class, for a teacher needs to know his class and be aware of his own ability to handle the material and the questions and discussion that may be discovered during the course of a lesson with a particular class. Material chosen ought to evoke an excited or thoughtful response, a vivid sense of experience, triggering off memories and evoking new experiences. So we have found ourselves reading aloud in class, or giving to pupils for their private reading, such books as Laura Ingalls Wilder's *Little House in the Big Woods*; *Little House on the Prairie*; *On the Banks of Plum Creek*; *By the Shores of Silver Lake*; E. B. White's *Charlotte's Web*; Rosemary Sutcliffe's *Dragon Slayer*;

Clive King's *Stig of the Dump*; Alan Garner's *The Moon of Gomrath*; *Elidor*; *The Owl Service*; Frederick Grice's *The Bonny Pit Laddie*; James Vance Marshall's *Walkabout*; Stan Barstow's *Joby*; Bill Naughton's short stories and Liam O'Flaherty's short stories. We have used also Moira Doolan's B.B.C. *Listening and Writing* booklets, as well as Conrad, Lawrence, Hemingway, Saroyan, Dylan Thomas, Richard Hughes, Homer, Gorki, Tolstoy, Grimm, Andrew Lang, Twain, and Dickens, up to the fourth-year classes.

These books are representative of the class libraries of paperback books that all the mixed-ability forms up to the fourth year have in their classroom. We have attempted to grade the paperbacks for their suitability to each year and to take account of an unstreamed form. One of six lessons each week is given over to individual reading. There are group discussions on the books, short extracts are read for class discussion, or there is a serialized reading aloud to the class, creative writing, improvised drama, or project work. Because we aim at a unitary, contextual, rather than a fragmented approach to our English teaching, the lessons are less preformulated than they might otherwise be and tend to move freely from reading to discussion, writing, or acting.

When reading, say, Grice's *The Bonny Pit Laddie*, using record-player, tape-recorder, photographs, and newspaper cuttings, the class can move from the teacher's reading of Grice's account of the pit-strike, the candymen, the pit accident, on to contemporary accounts of mining disasters like those of the Oaks Colliery, Barnsley, of 1866, Hindley Green Collieries, and Maypole Colliery, Wigan, in 1868 and 1908 respectively. We use poems by F. C. Boden, D. H. Lawrence, George Barker, Vernon Watkins and Ted Hughes; from *The Iron Muse*, edited by A. L. Lloyd for Topic Records, there are *The Durham Lockout*, *The Donibristle Moss Moran Disaster*, *Up the Raw*, *The Collier's Rant*, *The Blackleg Miners*; ballads and folk songs from *The Common Muse* edited by V. de Sola Pinto, and A. E. Rodway (Penguin); *The Avondale Mine Disaster*; *The Gresford Disaster*; *Come all ye bold miners*, by A. L. Lloyd; *Come all you gallant colliers*, by Ewan MacColl; *The Oak and the Ash*, by Frederick Grice; *The Whinstone Drift*, by Richard Armstrong; *Down the Mine*, by George Orwell; *Odour of Chrsyanthemums*, and extracts from *Sons and Lovers*, by D. H. Lawrence.

Or, if the book is James Vance Marshall's *Walkabout*, the reading can strike off into directions of talk, writing, drama, which will take in poetry from the Penguin books of *Australian Ballads*, and *Australian Verse*; poems by Ian Mudie, W. Hart-Smith, Judith Wright, David Campbell, Nancy Cato, Nan McDonald; transportation ballads, folk songs about Ned Kelly, songs from the bush and outback in *Outback Ballads*, Topic Records; *Aborigine*, by Hugo Williams; *Kangaroo Tales* (Puffin); *Journey Among Men*, by Marshall and Drysdale (Hodder and Stoughton); and films, film strips and slides available from Western Australia House, London.

Work of this kind can be either short-lived or extended over a long period of time depending upon the pupils' enthusiasm, and the teacher's awareness of its possibilities, and it can extend into a programme of entertainment for the whole school, where the object primarily is to give one another pleasure and not to compete: each house, or group of children, selects a theme to illustrate by song, dance, poem, prose and music; they evaluate the contributions, collaborate, and make decisions on the programme they want to present. Although this kind of approach can so easily be fitted into the teaching of a class as a whole, in an unstreamed class the significant teaching unit is the small group, preferably with the same teacher over a period of years, the pupils forming close personal relationships. The classroom then becomes more of a workshop where a number of self-chosen groups of children of varied interests and abilities, working under the teacher's guidance, are given a different assignment which is related to a larger topic to be produced in project form in a book, on tape, or as a wall display.

By using the terms, 'topic' or 'project', I may seem to imply that there is always at the outset a systematic arrangement of material and pre-planning of lessons over a long period, but this need not be the case. From a pupil grumbling about a school dinner, or from a reading of a Hemingway description of eating outdoors, can come excited descriptions by the pupils of favourite meals, and a 'project' can be under way. In the course of the lesson the teacher and the pupils may discover many possible avenues that an apparently inconsequential discussion has created. The project will be given a name, but probably only when all the work is collected together; meanwhile the pupils will have been concerned in many activities, and may have shared, through literature, in many other experiences.

Orwell's descriptions of working in a restaurant in *Down and Out in Paris and London*; fables concerned with greed by La Fontaine; limericks, rhymes; jokes in the Opies' *The Lore and Language of Schoolchildren*; *World of the Child* (Penguin); *Oliver Twist*; extracts from *Corduroy*, by A. Bell; *Lark Rise to Candleford*, by F. Thompson; *Mr. Clifford's Good English*, by J. H. Walsh; *Don't Knock the Corners Off*, by C. Glyn; *Big Two-Hearted River*, by Hemingway; short stories by Bill Naughton, for example, 'Seventeen Oranges', 'Gift of the Gab'; *The Truth about Pyecraft*, by H. G. Wells; the strange eating customs in 'Eating with the Howeitat' from T. E. Lawrence's *Seven Pillars of Wisdom*; *The Boy Who Wouldn't Play Jesus*, by Bernard Kops; *Mulcaster Market*, by James Reeves; voracious animals and birds in short stories by Liam O'Flaherty, and poems by Ted Hughes and Edmund Blunden; Dylan Thomas's description of a Christmas dinner; Chaucer's portraits of the Prioresse, Frankeleyn, and Cook; Edwin

Brock's 'Song of the Battery Hen'; the poems of Seamus Heaney; 'Hot Cake', by Shu Hsi; J. A. Lindon's 'Sink Song'; 'Apples' by Laurie Lee; 'After Apple-Picking', by Robert Frost; 'Shoals of Herring', by Ewan MacColl; 'John Barleycorn'; 'Ground-Hog'; and even, perhaps, the symbolic fear of the forbidden fruit and 'eating the object' in Blake's 'A Poison Tree'—this would be some of the literature read to the class as a whole, or by individuals, or by groups. Groups and individuals will be involved in working on interviews with the school cook, a report on school meals; analyzing advertisements for food and preparing an exhibition of the work of Oxfam, a comparison in montage of 'the haves and the have-nots'. There will be group plays and opportunities for writing in free verse, short stories, descriptions, scripts for tape on animals and birds of prey, eating out in an expensive restaurant, at a polite Aunt's, a birthday party, the family at breakfast, washing up, preparing a meal for a very special occasion, a pie-eating contest, the perfect meal, picnic, a greedy person and a fussy, finicky person, being famished, unpleasant food, strange and exotic foods, predators, the butcher's shop, a supermarket, mother's kitchen, making bread, battery chickens, 'scrumping' apples.

There can be single lessons or a sequence of lessons where all the separable English skills of reading, modes of writing and discourse, drama, can be used as the need arises, as occasions present themselves, to illuminate a central topic or interest. By encouraging mutual criticism by the pupils of each other's work, by not dwelling on faults at the expense of gaining the trust of the pupils and showing sympathetic interest in their efforts, they are more naturally concerned with improving the accuracy and effectiveness of their work, and they are more ready and willing to improve their basic skills in writing. The 'polishing' of the work in progress is seen as a genuine need before it is presented to the teacher and the rest of the class.

Much of this work will mean that pupils will be moving from individual study, to work in small groups, as well as working for part of the time with the whole class. The teacher's role will be to provide opportunities for informal discussion in small groups—in the early days the teacher leads the discussion but gradually allows the pupils to take over more fully. At times, class discussion can operate as a result of spontaneous interests in the class or the teacher. This helps the pupils to question, listen, qualify, elaborate, collaborate and accommodate themselves to others: in an unstreamed class this involves children of all abilities, backgrounds, ranges of vocabulary, interests, points of view, in reviewing their own and others' responses, sharing in a creative activity, forming new friendships, and valuing in each other not only intelligence, but also humour, patience, perseverance, in the give and take of the group or class as a whole. The only rule is that they should not all talk at once but learn how to 'interrupt', how to talk with one another. It is this kind of discussion that we aim at, rather than the more formal debate or prepared speech which pupils can be very keen on at first (as with the initial glamorous attraction of stage, costume, and 'showing off' in drama work) but although these can be used profitably in the fourth year and later, even then one must guard against 'one-upmanship' and a competitive aggression to score easy points. Rather than controversy for its own sake we expect and hope for the interchange of a variety of points of view, a diversity of language, the social art of listening and respect for others.

One can create congenial groups and the enthusiastic sociometrist can attempt to nullify incipient conflict within a group by manipulating and arranging groups; or groups can be allowed to come together by choice. Class organization, which becomes increasingly important in group work, and the conflicts which arise, whether or not the groups are pre-planned, can be faced by the pupils who with tactful help from the teacher can learn the valuable lesson of coming to terms with what they can do to each other. There is a fairly frequent disruption in a group in the first or even second year when one child is cast out of the group—but the whole group can have the chance of working through the difficulties and making amends for irritating and disturbing one another. The members of the group can become more sensitive to each other's needs but to do so they will need to have the trust of the teacher who will have to encourage them to be as honest with him as he is with them. The pupils will have to examine their motives for behaviour and feelings more honestly while the teacher, through literature, drama, discussion, and the pupils' personal descriptions of actual experience, aims to bring these problems out into the open and if it is to do with 'outsiders'—the lonely, the rejects, the bullies, the cowards, the 'good boy', the 'square', the 'teacher's pet', the 'show-off', the timid, the exuberant, the fun-loving, the coquette, the joker—to do so without making specific reference to the living examples in the class itself. In a free, undirected discussion, or in more concerted thought about a play, novel, or poem, we may be reflecting some emotional problem that concerns our relationship with another. It is only an extension of this to ask the pupils to move, vicariously, into similar situations in literature, thus extending their range of experience and their understanding.

The practical arrangement of the classroom itself is important when one is concerned with facility of movement from one activity to another within the lesson. At Settle the English rooms, apart from the library, are kept close together for interchange of books and audio-visual aids and classes in drama and project work. The layout of the desks and chairs in the rooms is U-shaped to allow for quick and easy re-arrangement of desks for improvised drama, discussion in groups, for groups taking turns to be the audience, for whole-class discussion during or after a reading or writing task. A desk for the teacher or for a group of six pupils completes the 'circle' and the rest of the 'circle' is double-tiered with girls on chairs in front and boys sitting on desks behind. The actual process of communication between pupils, and between pupils and teacher, is affected by the physical arrangements of furniture in the different activities of the English lesson, and by not always being teacher-centred the flexible strategy of arrangement encourages, for example, the shy children to become more articulate instead of relying on the other pupils or the teacher.

One of the difficulties which arises when the class is unstreamed and the pupils are likely to be working variously as individuals, in small groups, or as a class is that it is necessary to have ready to hand a mass of material for the pupils to use and study. The problem is not so much the lack of material but the collecting and controlling of a burgeoning variety of materials. We have found ourselves having a growing impatience with text-books which, however stimulating in their content and format, have by their very form and nature a too restrictive, cut-and-dried lack of immediacy and freshness about them. This is not a retreat from the printed word, but an awareness in class of the inhibition that a text-book can create: the media through which we learn should be also a means of self-expression. We do not use text-books but make heavy use of a duplicating machine and spend much time finding the right poem for the right occasion. Especially useful are folders or packs of material concerned with a topic and consisting of pamphlets, separate prose extracts from literature, poems, photographs, newspaper cuttings, prints, manuscripts, facsimiles, broadsheets, film loops, tapes, gramophone records, which leave room for the addition of the children's own writing and discoveries. The teacher must be free to find his own material to add to the lessons, since the teacher's enthusiasms will frequently stimulate the involvement of the class.

For example, such a folder could well be made about the school. 'School' as a topic can arouse surprising interest in both those who are bored by the institution and those who are fully involved in it; as a subject it gives an opportunity to the teacher for making real contact with the children. The amount of relevant literature is vast and there are plenty of activities that could be designed to present moral or psychological situations and problems in discussion groups or for the acting out of roles. It is a subject which can move in many different directions beyond 'school', into 'growing up', 'childhood', 'authority', as the imagination makes its connections and memories are suddenly recalled. The literature need not be rendered merely functional, as a 'teaching aid'; the topic for discussion or dramatic improvisation is usually inspired by the literature, then texts or parts of texts come to mind to throw light on an aspect of the theme or open up another area for consideration as the topic takes off. The language of any of the literature read can be given close scrutiny and critically evaluated; the literature can act as a springboard for the pupils' own writing, but there will be occasions when a poem or short story is best left to itself without a rigorous determination to ransack it for its momentary usefulness. This literature includes *One Small Boy*, by B. Naughton; *Don't Knock the Corners Off*, by C. Glyn; *Portrait of the Artist as a Young Man*, by James Joyce; David's arrival at Creakle's school in *David Copperfield*, *Nicholas Nickleby*, and *Hard Times*, by Dickens; *Joby*, by S. Barstow, and the short story 'One of the Virtues' by the same author; *Radcliffe*, by David Storey; *Lark Rise to Candleford*, by F. Thompson; *This Time Next Week*, by L. Thomas; *There is a Happy Land*, by K. Waterhouse; *Enemies of Promise*, by C. Connolly; *The Teachers*, by G. W. Target; *Up the Down Staircase*, by B. Kaufmann; *The Bonny Pit Laddie*, by Frederick

Grice; *Cider With Rosie*, by Laurie Lee; *Village School*, by 'Miss Read'; *An education of a coster lad*, by Mayhew; *Huckleberry Finn* and *Tom Sawyer*, by Twain; *Roaring Boys*, by E. Blishen; *A Precocious Autobiography*, by Y. Yevtushenko; *The Rainbow*, by D. H. Lawrence; *World of the Child* (Penguin books); novels of William Mayne; short stories by W. Golding, W. Saroyan, D. Thomas; poems by John Walsh—'William and Susan', 'The New Boy', 'The Truants', 'I've got an apple ready', 'The Bully Asleep', 'From the classroom window'—in *The Truants* (Heinemann) and in the B.B.C. pamphlets *Listening and Writing*; 'Last lesson of the afternoon', by D. H. Lawrence; 'The Playground', in *The Excitement of Writing*; 'I wake up in the morning', in *The Keen Edge*, by J. Beckett; 'The Fool of the Class', in *Presenting Poetry* (Methuen); 'Milk', in *Poetry 2, Key of the Kingdom*; *The Lore and Language of Schoolchildren*, by I. and P. Opie; *Children's Games*, by D. Holbrook; 'Timothy Winters', by C. Causley; 'My Parents Kept me from children who were rough', by S. Spender; 'Holiday', by Julian Mitchell; 'The Lesson', by E. Lucie-Smith; 'Out of School', by Hal Summers; 'Lies', by Y. Yevtushenko; *David and Broccoli*, by J. Mortimer; *Ars Longa, Vita Brevis*, by J. Arden and M. D'Arcy; *Unman, Wittering and Zigo*, by Giles Cooper; *A Kestrel for a Knave*, by Barry Hines (Penguin); *The African Child*, by Camara Laye (Fontana); *School remembered*, ed. Gillian Avery (Gollancz); and *The School I'd like*, ed. Edward Blishen (Penguin).

The topics that will arise out of this reading and listening are many and varied and will take the form of individual, group, or class work, writing, discussion, tape-recording, interviewing, letter-writing, and improvised drama dealing with: school assembly and being named or rebuked in public, receiving a prize or trophy, performing in the choir, reading a lesson, day-dreaming, speech day, open day; visitors to school, to lessons, the school dentist, optician, doctor, parents' visits; being called to the headmaster's study; first day at school; school meals, school milk break; the playground; teacher's pet, the bully, cheat, coward; 'splitting', 'sneaking', stealing, truancy; unfair punishment; name-calling; making friends, breaking friends, quarrels, fights; school bus, on the way to school, on the way home from school; in real trouble; the good times; the classroom when the teacher is not there; working on surveys and questionnaires on uniform, smoking, homework, punishment, discipline, school rules, friendship patterns within the school; comparing and contrasting comics or novels featuring life at school with the real thing; making collages of photographs of school with accompanying prose and poems; drafting notes for assembly, instructions on firedrill, designing notices for school meetings, conducting visitors around school; an unruly class; teachers; co-education.

DRAMA

We make a distinction between drama and theatre and regard them as two quite distinct activities in the sense that we assume that drama and the development of the child as a person are intimately related: we are not training the children as professional actors, nor is the school play regarded as a natural progression of the work in drama done in the department. Our work in drama, as with our teaching in general, is not only concerned with the naturally gifted few who can assume with some skill the theatrical conventions, but also with the majority, and drama, like discussion and writing and the other activities of the English lesson, is just one other means of exploring and ordering experience. Drama is not regarded as a separate subject, but another activity: we avoid the lure of giving it the order of a systematized syllabus which would dwell on theatrical history, stage and costume design, for example. Drama is concerned with developing people and whilst the double period of eighty minutes each week is devoted to it, drama can just as easily be slotted into five- or ten-minute periods, spontaneously.

The showing and distribution of photographs, newspaper cuttings, pictures from magazines, advertisements, postcard reproductions of paintings, the children's own paintings and sketches done in art lessons, the use of drum, gong, cymbal, recorded music, which can be used for individual imaginative writing, or a reading of, say, the Icarus myth, Cyclops, *Beowulf, Sir Gawayne and the Green Knight*, can all be used as stimuli for improvised drama. The class can divide up into pairs or small groups of six, or can start as a whole class, with discussion first and then improvisation. There will be drama exercises in concentration and observation, using the five senses, of the kind suggested by Brian Way in *Development through Drama* (Longmans, 1967). The stimulation of the imagination will begin by taking advantage of what already exists, what the children bring with them into the class: if the whole class is taking part in a drama lesson in the hall then there can be a central situation, a railway-station, Youth Club, dance, cafe, supermarket, market place, into which conflict can be introduced. Working in pairs, and eventually in groups, there will be family quarrels over hire-purchase, watching television, the boyfriend and girlfriend; the roles of liar, thief, bully, cheat, pompous man; visits to patients in hospital, to elderly or infirm people, to relations, interviews for jobs, facing up to salesmen, making complaints. Many of the early activities will take place with the class as a whole taking part in a large area, then the pupils can work in pairs, and then in groups when confidence emerges so that eventually there is a collection of individual efforts, stimulated by exchange of ideas and suggestions during the group preparation and activity so that the children are helping each other and learning to live with each other and working together.

This simplifies the reality, of course, and a problem of improvisation is the danger of 'strengthening the self-assertive, and weakening the insecure' with the deprived child, for instance, constantly cast by the group in a comic role: the social interaction and problems of groups working together in drama are examined in *Group Drama*, D. E. Adland (Longmans, 1964). There would seem to be no correlation between academic intelligence and ability in drama and since drama does not *depend* on scripts (there are usually only a few pupils in even a top stream who can read a script with fluency and characterization, and the topics for improvised drama are only infrequently available in script form anyway) the work of mixed-ability groups in drama provides a great opportunity for extending sympathy and understanding amongst children of all kinds from different social backgrounds—mixed ability is seen to work in action in drama groups.

The results of a mixed-ability group performing a group play based on a family situation—at the breakfast table, should the grandmother live with the family? boyfriend/girlfriend brought home for the first time, winning the 'pools', new baby, first job—can be devastating and almost irreconcilable as one mode of speech and code of behaviour conflicts with another. No specific instructions are given on whether they should act as their own parents behave, or act in a way quite different; the criteria on which discussion will start will be: could this happen, is this how people behave, would they react in this way; then, should they behave and react in this way, why do they behave and speak like this? The first lessons in improvised drama can be a shambles with a total lack of order and pupils diverted from their main intentions, all talking at once; they depend for their improvement and progress on the right timing of the introduction of critical comment either from the teacher or the pupils. The first essentials are the building of confidence and trust and freedom from criticism and competition. Playing to the class audience by a group that receives praise and suggestions can come later when insincerity, shyness and self-consciousness have been overcome to some extent.

There is a very early demand for costumes which is best limited to one garment or property to each person, sufficient to stimulate improvisation and establish character, e.g. a hat, pipe, walking-stick, newspaper, a mask, a cloak. Anything more than this can become a device which becomes more important than anything else.

Just as poor spelling, obscure handwriting, lack of form and precision in written work can interfere with and even destroy its content, so in drama there is at first dialogue out of character, dialogue inadequately establishing the situation, arguments which become slanging-matches taking place out of context, plays which have no beginning, middle, or end. The teacher, by assuming an unobtrusive role, helps each group in turn in their preparation by fostering relevant and friendly discussion, by being critical but enthusiastic in rehearsal, and surprisingly soon the group absorption in an enjoyable, creative effort makes the earlier, thorough organization and control less necessary. As the groups become more self-reliant the class as a whole becomes more self-critical and concerned with accuracy of observation, authenticity, and more involved in the improvised plays they either take part in or observe, so learning to meet a variety of situations, to take on a variety of roles, to assume different modes of language.

Fully scripted plays written by the pupils themselves seldom work very well, as the children stumble and get impatient of the restrictions, and they are best used as 'radio plays' or programmes on tape. But improvising without a script can lead to drama with a script, and is, I think, an essential preparation for an intelligent and worth-while reading or acting-out of dramatic texts. We have found that pupils who otherwise would have stumbled depressingly through a part in a scripted play can, because of early practice in their own group plays, read and act a part in a play with a fluency and interpretation which become essential in the fifth and sixth forms as a prelude to the close study of a dramatic text.

EXAMINATIONS: C.S.E. MODE 3, G.C.E.

There are no examinations in English in the first four years at the school, and no marks or form-lists are required; there are just brief, conventional termly reports plus regular parental access to staff opinion on a pupil's achievements in relation to the average of the year-group. In English at the Certificate of Secondary Education level we have our own school syllabus in Mode 3—we can decide what we want to teach and the way we want to teach it, and in conjunction with an outside moderator we award the grades in the assessment at the end of the two-year course. We can try to ensure that the content of the course is best suited to the individual pupils taking the course, and if we do not succeed in doing this we cannot blame anonymous examiners or examination boards.

The approach and content of the work are on very similar lines to those of the earlier years in the school: we move from writing and discussion of individual experience to the world of the family, the neighbourhood, employment, and the wider human issues of old age, illness, marriage, war, education, and try to encourage a clearer and more complex understanding by the pupils of their society. Each pupil has a folder in which he or she keeps written and illustrative work of all kinds: creative writing in poetry, prose, dramatic dialogue, topic work and diaries. The stress is not so much on the acquisition of information, recording of facts, colourful presentation and illustration, as on how successfully the pupil has rendered the topic valid to him or her, explored its implications, the growth of understanding it has brought about, and the degree of success with which language has been used to express all this adequately. For example, incorporated into the course-work presented for assessment in the C.S.E. English are the 'work-experience' diaries or journals: these are the result of an arrangement whereby pupils spend two or three weeks in conditions of full-time out-of-school employment as shop assistants, in hairdressing, garage workshops, farm-work, a residential school for handicapped children, hotel kitchen work, and the like, in addition to other visits and observations at places of work. The pupils' findings and experiences are written up and discussed, and the material is used in lessons on work and leisure. They will use their own direct experiences however brief, interviews with parents, ex-pupils and outside speakers, together with literature.

There are no literature set-books as such, for most of the literature read will either arise from pursuing the individual, group, or class topic and will, therefore, be either programmed or unrestricted, or the literature will come from a 'free range' reading programme from their paperback class-library supplemented by a reading list of suggested books. A relatively small number of texts will be given close study over a longer period of time, depending upon a particular teacher or class enthusiasm, or circumstance; for example, a reading of *The Lord of the Flies* would be accompanied by a showing of the film, discussion, and extended topic work using drama. The literature set aside for the C.S.E. examination contains, in addition to about eighty individual paperbacks, such books as: Wesker's *Roots*; Waterhouse and Hall's *Billy Liar* and *The Long, The Short, and The Tall*; Shakespeare's *Julius Caesar, Macbeth, Coriolanus*, and *Romeo and Juliet*; *Worth a Hearing*, edited by A. Bradley; *Hobson's Choice*, by H. Brighouse; poems of Clare, Edward Thomas, Owen, Lawrence, Frost, Larkin, Hughes; Sillitoe's *The Loneliness of the Long Distance*

Runner, *Saturday Night and Sunday Morning*, and short stories; Steinbeck's *The Pearl* and *The Grapes of Wrath*; Graves's *Goodbye to All That*; Hemingway's *The Old Man and the Sea*; Twain's *Huckleberry Finn* and *Puddn'head Wilson*; Conrad's *The Nigger of the 'Narcissus'*, *Shadow Line*, and *Typhoon*; Hughes's *A High Wind in Jamaica*; Lee's *Cider With Rosie*; Dickens's *Great Expectations*; Barstow's *A Kind of Loving*, and short stories; E. Brontë's *Wuthering Heights*; H. Lee's *To Kill a Mocking Bird*; and books by Orwell, Lawrence, Liam O'Flaherty, Bill Naughton, Isaac Babel, and Sid Chaplin.

Fifty percent of the final assessment is based on the course-work. In the internal examination at the end of the second year the pupils are required to come to terms with a passage from a novel or drama (in the recent past, from *Huckleberry Finn*, *Sons and Lovers*, *Roots*), show an understanding of its essential matter, and use the passage as a starting-point for a piece of writing of their own. They are also required to use language in a more objective, expository manner—a report, a letter, a critical analysis of the language of advertising and propaganda. In addition there will be a more extended piece of writing of an imaginative, creative kind where there will be an attempt in the formulation of the topic to engage the interest of the candidate by a series of points, lengthy quotation, or more tangible stimulus: a painting, photograph, poem, or piece of music, rather than simply giving a title which can all too easily encourage the facile, uninvolved writing we are not concerned with. There is, finally, an oral examination in which after reading aloud a passage of prose the pupil discusses a pre-selected topic with the teacher/assessor. We should like, for the future, to find some means by which we could incorporate into the assessment the lively course activity by the pupils in improvised and scripted drama.

As for the G.C.E., the new revised syllabus in English language and literature at Ordinary level of the Northern

Universities Joint Matriculation Board, and the same board's experiment in school assessment at O-level, are encouraging; but for the future we place our hopes in a C.S.E. Mode 3 examination, extended to include the present fifth-form G.C.E. pupils, and the development of an internally controlled examination of the C.S.E. type for pupils at eighteen either to complement or replace the present A-level examination.

THE NON-EXAMINATION FOURTH FORM

It is already difficult, and will become even more so with the raising of the school-leaving age, to prevent the non-examination pupils from being outsiders in any school system operating for the more able child. We attempt at the moment to avoid both a watered-down academic curriculum, and a situation in which several enlightened but specialist subject teachers have little opportunity of getting a wider view of these pupils' particular needs. One teacher acts as a tutor, form teacher and careers adviser, as well as teaching his subject. For instance, this year, being an English Department colleague, he teaches six periods of English each week together with lessons in General Studies, and participates in an afternoon each week given over to projects. The form see their teacher in more than one kind of learning situation; the formroom becomes their room; there is an interdependence between formroom activities and the subjects taught by the same teacher; activities which at first can be regarded as very much 'school work' can develop into hobbies and voluntary enterprises; and the tutor can follow his pupils' development closely both in school and as they make their approach to the working world.

The school's C.S.E. English course is sufficiently flexible and open-ended to allow the teacher of the school-leavers in the fourth year to teach them appropriately in the same spirit so that a number of these pupils who remain for a further year can continue to follow the course for a grade at C.S.E. The English teacher might also deal, in a project system which becomes interdisciplinary, with current affairs and their historical and geographical background, local government, municipal and social organization and relevant local history, rates, tax, public health, as well as homemaking, marriage, families, personal relations, love and interdependence, youth and old age, in conjunction with other teachers in other subject departments of the school. As with the work-experience project at C.S.E. the pupils undertake a similar project to do with a job or trade. Also, if the time-table can be made flexible enough, and depending upon staff availability and room, the pupils could be allowed to spend more extended periods of time doing work of their own choice with wood, metal, clay, paint, drama, film, tape, cooking, dressmaking, gardening, photography, looking after animals, playing, singing or listening to music.

In addition to having enough money for buying the books that we want to use in school, it would not be too difficult to make out a case for the essential need of: a drama workshop, departmental secretarial help, a videotape machine, tape-recorders, record-players, a printing press, a ciné-camera. More important than these, though, is the opportunity for a teacher of English to share in the mutual exchange of ideas, encouragement, and experience with his immediate colleagues at a local teachers' centre, and with university and college of education departments, so that by being in a position to evaluate the development of new ideas, approaches and materials, and by refreshing his own study of literature and knowledge of film, television, radio, fine art, and drama, he will be more likely to be able to cope with the tensions of teaching English at the present time, take part more fully in continuing his own education and, accordingly, that of the pupils he meets in his classroom.

English in an urban setting: Churchfields Comprehensive School, West Bromwich

ANTHONY ADAMS

Churchfields School is a large comprehensive school of nearly 2,000 pupils, both boys and girls, on the 'green-belt' fringe of West Bromwich. It was built as a purpose-built comprehensive some twelve years ago and normally takes all pupils in its catchment area above the E.S.N. (educationally sub-normal) range.

A system of entry has been devised by the local education authority whereby pupils in the catchment area go to Churchfields as by right; they can, however, opt to take the 11+ examination, in which case they go either to the authority's grammar school or one of the secondary modern schools. Any vacant places amongst the entry are filled by pupils from other parts of the borough who have applied for a place there and whose 11+ score is the same as that of one of the pupils who has opted out. In this way it is hoped to preserve the principle of parental choice and to maintain the comprehensive principle itself. In practice, over recent years, there has been an increasing tendency for pupils in the catchment area to opt for the school, but there is no doubt that the existence of the grammar school does 'cream' Churchfields entry to some extent.

From September 1969, however, a scheme of secondary school reorganization has been implemented and all the schools are now organized on comprehensive lines. This has entailed, amongst other things, a redrawing of the catchment areas and will eventually produce in consequence some comprehensives with a very 'privileged' entry and others which will tend to be very depressed. It is unlikely that Churchfields will be much affected except that 'creaming' will no longer take place. The number of immigrant children in the school can also be expected to increase.

West Bromwich is an intellectually deprived area with something below the national spread of I.Q. amongst the school population. The result is that although the school receives the occasional very brilliant pupil, its intake tends to be depressed in this respect; my experience in grammar schools makes me suspect that Churchfields entry does not normally contain more than about fifteen pupils a year of what would be regarded as A-stream grammar-school ability.

The school is in a well-to-do working-class area. Very few of the pupils are deprived in a material sense and most of them live on a local authority housing estate in reasonably affluent conditions in an area of full employment. They are, however, culturally very deprived. There is little respect for education locally amongst the parents and few of the homes will contain books of any kind. The opportunities for employment mean that many of the pupils leave school as soon as they can and in consequence the sixth form is small in comparison with the size of the school as a whole. There is no parents' association and very little involvement by the parents in the life of the school. It is in fact the exceptional parent who ever comes into the school once his child has started there. Homework is a difficulty: there is little sympathy with it at home and little opportunity for the average pupil to work in any reasonable conditions at home. The general attitude of the pupils is a friendly one; there is little resentment or hostility to school. On the other hand there is also little evidence of any real spirit of involvement. The children will cooperate with teachers quite willingly but they nonetheless find many of their attitudes alien and unintelligible.

The school is organized on a house system, the houses being physically distinguished by being in different blocks. Each house is run by a housemaster who is responsible for something like 200 pupils. The house is the school's basic social unit. Pupils register and dine in houses and the housemasters and house tutors have pastoral responsibility for their pupils; the policy is that each house should contain a complete cross-section of the school's intake.

The academic side of the school is quite separate from the houses, and is controlled by the heads of departments who have considerable freedom to run their departments as they please under the overall control of the headmaster. House blocks during teaching time become teaching blocks and each major department centres its work on a particular block, although large departments, such as English, have to spill out into other blocks as well. This system involves difficulties which will be dealt with later.

The basic policy of the school is one of setting for individual subjects. Pupils are put into 'general sets' in the first three years in which they take such subjects as Games, Religious Education, Art and Craft. For the major academic subjects they are set separately by ability in terms of that subject—that is, English, Mathematics, Modern Languages, Science, are set for each year across the whole year time-table so that heads of departments are able to set their pupils according to their own requirements. Normally this setting is done for ability in the particular subject concerned, although the policy of the English Department is against setting by ability and in recent years there has been in this subject a determined move towards mixed-ability setting, hostile to the general ethos of the school though this is. In the first year, the Head of English and the deputy headmistress are jointly responsible for the assignment of pupils to their general sets, based upon a battery of tests taken shortly after entry to the school. In the past there was an attempt to create something like twelve graduated sets each year; it is now recognized that this is not a practical possibility and the setting instead is in broad bands of ability. In addition to the setting in the main school there is a separate Remedial Department which is normally reduced by a set each year as children leave the Remedial Department in order to join the main school. There is at present close personal contact between the Head of Remedial and the Head of English, although the latter has no direct control over the work that goes on in the Remedial Department. There has recently been a welcome move towards the Remedial Department becoming a 'clinic' with pupils being withdrawn from the normal setting for remedial work as needed.

In the fourth and fifth years the policy is one of allocating pupils to specific, vocationally based, courses. Thus there is an 'Options' (academically based) course, a course in Commerce (including shorthand and typing), an Accounts course and so on—English continues to be taught to all pupils and continues its policy of independent setting so that the vocationally based courses do not affect the subject directly. The policy of the English Department is to enter all pupils remaining for a fifth year for some kind of external examination. About 60 pupils (two sets) are entered each year for O-level English language and literature, and about 100 for English in C.S.E. A number of able pupils leave on the completion of the fifth-form course and the sixth form rarely numbers more than 30 each year. Of these the English Department would normally expect to receive between twelve and fifteen pupils each year as candidates for A-level English. There is no General English as such time-tabled for the sixth forms, although there is a General Studies course to which some member of the English Department normally makes a contribution. Some sixth-form linguistics is now being experimented with and the school is one of the testing institutions for the Schools Council Linguistics Project.

Most of the pupils live at a distance of several miles from the school; this makes for a late start to the school day (9.20 a.m.) and also means that the organization of out-of-school activities is difficult. Thus there is little in the way of after-school clubs, considering the size of the school. A notable exception in this respect is the Theatre Workshop, run by a member of the English Department, which is a drama club meeting weekly and engaging in a variety of dramatic activities leading to a number of lunchtime productions each term and also to a major annual production. Drama is organized in this way on an ensemble basis in the school and the idea of the annual production as a separate prestige-making activity is frowned upon. Theatre Workshop has a long-term planned policy so that although at the time of writing we have just finished our production of *Bartholomew Fair* (Ben Jonson), next spring's production of Brecht's *Mother Courage* has already been in mind for some time. There is also to be a German tour in the summer of John Arden's *The Royal Pardon*. Theatre Workshop is run by a committee of teachers with the Head of English as chairman and deliberately seeks to involve a large number of pupils and staff who may have other interests than pure acting. Thus there is a section concerned with stage design and lighting, a publicity section, and so on. Of the out-of-school societies there is no doubt that Theatre Workshop is the most successful and involves something like 150 pupils most of the time. Its success is due almost entirely to the interest, enthusiasm and expertise of a particular teacher who has described his work at length in a recent book,[1] but it does suggest that more out-of-school activities could be conducted, given the enthusiasm, and that the 'bus problem' is an excuse rather than a reason for our timidity in this respect.

The high employment locally means that there is little need to gear the activities of the schools in the direction of particular

[1] Robert Leach, *Theatre for Youth* (Pergamon Press, 1970).

local industries, although the fourth- and fifth-year courses are very largely vocationally based. It remains true, however, that for most of the pupils and their parents, education is a means towards a job rather than anything else.

As already stated most of the English teaching is conducted in one of the house blocks although it is necessary to have some English classrooms elsewhere. This means that the English Department is a highly centralized body for the most part and the head of department is able to keep a very close watch on what exactly is going on. The full-time members of the department will normally have tea together at break and there is in the block staff-room a continuous and animated discussion of curriculum and methods. This has an undoubted value as far as the morale of the department is concerned. The English block consists of conventional classrooms although there is a conscious policy of trying to break up the formal classroom atmosphere. Thus the old-fashioned desks are arranged in groups rather than in rows to encourage group work and discussion amongst the pupils and gradually these are being replaced by stackable tables and chairs which can easily be adapted to a variety of patterns to fit different teaching situations.

Each house block has its own dining room and these spaces get used for drama work although they are not entirely satisfactory since the work has frequently to be carried out against a background of washing-up noises from the kitchen. However, the space is very valuable, especially as the two halls that the school also possesses are generally being used for Physical Education work and so are not readily available to the English Department for drama work. There is a policy of using a good deal of visual material in English lessons although to show a film requires considerable organization. The situation is somewhat improved now that there is a black-out in one of the rooms in the English teaching block, but there is only one projector available in the whole school and that has to be shifted from room to room. There is a real need for the provision of more adequate visual teaching facilities in the school and, in particular, the provision of a properly equipped projection room. Unfortunately, the importance of this element of education is not properly appreciated either by the authority or by the headmaster and the money allowed for film hire and for the servicing of equipment is minimal in consequence. It is also possible to borrow for specific periods on application to the master in charge of visual aids such things as a strip and slide projector and a television set; none of this equipment is owned by the English Department itself.

The department does possess three tape-recorders, including a portable model, and also a record-player. There is a fairly wide selection of records which have to be bought out of the normal capitation allowance. Access to an 8 mm. film camera is also available although many members of staff prefer to use their own Super-8 equipment: the only thing stopping further experiment along these lines is the cost of film stock which again has to be paid for out of capitation—as indeed does tape for the tape-recorder.

The provision of money is a considerable problem and the capitation allowance is far too small for the needs of a department of this size. It has to be kept in mind that the provision of O- and A-level books for the fifth and sixth forms must run away with a considerable proportion of the capitation money each year. There is a constant shortage of basic materials in consequence—Sellotape, glue, coloured markers, sugar paper: the teaching policy of the department makes considerable demands upon these things and they are always in short supply to the frustration of staff and pupils alike. Books are fairly well provided for. There is a current policy of buying paperbacks since so many books are lost that their shorter life is not a serious problem and books will normally be bought either as individual copies or in short sets of twenty. There is rarely any need for the issue of the same book to all members of the class at any one time and the department policy is opposed to the class-reader system. With the limited resources that are available, our policy is to buy a large variety of books rather than many copies of any one title—poetry anthologies and modern drama texts exist in fair profusion. Stock is kept in store cupboards annexed to each of the teaching rooms and in the head of department's office.

One of the most pressing needs of the department is for its own duplicating equipment. A great deal of home-produced teaching material is employed and this has to be duplicated in the school office which is understaffed and overworked. The office staff is very cooperative although there is an inevitable delay in the production of material in consequence.

The head of department is fortunate in having his own office and a reasonable allowance of free periods (10) for departmental administration. There is a great deal of grumbling about the lack of facilities that the school provides although it is undoubtedly well off in comparison with many secondary schools in the area. However, it is astonishing that a school built so recently is so traditional in its design of teaching space and provision of facilities. This is proving particularly irksome in view of the experimental policy that the English Department is currently initiating, and a great deal of frustration results.

There is also a need for a good deal more provision of secretarial assistance. The head of department could well do with a part-time secretary of his own and is convinced that he must be the highest-paid stencil typist in the authority's service. The authority's failure to provide adequate secretarial assistance is both time-consuming and uneconomical.

The department at present consists of about twelve members, six of whom are full-time—the rest are shared with other departments. The full-time members of the department are nearly all graduates, although not all of them in English, and teach in the English block. There is a policy of assigning a teaching room to particular members of staff and the pupils move from room to room. Since the deparmtent has been fairly stable over the last three years there has been the opportunity to build up a corporate philosophy and unity of practice amongst department members. Of late there has been some successful experimenting with team-teaching (which will be described in more detail later) and the policy is one of democratic discussion with the head of department acting as chairman rather than of an autocratic imposition of a policy from above. There is a real need for an opportunity for the department to meet as a whole in school time; at present departmental meetings are held weekly in the lunch-hours but this is a considerable strain as the teachers frequently have house duties to perform in the lunch-hours also. In addition to formal departmental meetings there is a great deal of informal discussion in the staff-room of course, but this means a loss of effective contact with those members of the department who teach in other blocks. It is necessary therefore for the head of department to circulate administrative instructions in duplicated format which adds to the mass of paper that an individual teacher at the school may receive in the shape of circulars from headmaster, housemasters and heads of department. There does, however, seem to be in the school generally a distrust of office efficiency and this seems to be a major problem of the organization of a very large school. With the present move towards large schools some training in administrative procedures would seem to be a valuable thing to include in students' training.

There is little choice available so far as recruitment is concerned since the area is not generally a very attractive one to teachers. We have been lucky, however, in acquiring a strong team of young teachers who stay rather longer than one would expect: the department is therefore rather more stable than is normal in the school. The most recent acquisition is a young teacher who joined us in the autumn and who has specialist qualifications in linguistics—he has just completed an M.A. in this field. I regard this as a valuable acquisition to the team, although some of my colleagues are sceptical about the value of linguistics in English studies. There is, of course, no intention of introducing this into the curriculum, apart from the General Studies course in the sixth form, but it is hoped that the particular interests of this teacher will provide an added potentiality to the resources of the English team as a whole. The department is unquestionably viewed as a team, not only specifically so for some of its teaching, but in the way in which all major decisions are arrived at by a process of both formal and informal discussion. As in many other respects the department runs contrary to school policy here, the headmaster's approach and that of most other departments tending to be hierarchical.

The English syllabus was written five years ago and is now considerably out of date. It does state at the beginning, however, that the course is a literature-based one and that would still be the intention of most of the department members. This is one reason why graduates in English are generally the most valuable recruits to the department staff: there are a number of excellent History graduates that have taught English in the department and many of these are first-class teachers. In general, however, they are lacking in the breadth of reading that is essential if the right literary illustration for a particular teaching situation is to be easily found.

More and more the orientation of the teaching is towards group work and away from formal classroom instruction; the text-book has been outlawed altogether. The four basic activities on which the work is based are talk, drama, writing and reading and the work is largely organized in the form of projects in order to ensure an adequate coverage of all these elements. A great deal of use is made of duplicated sheets of instructions and 'job cards' which are issued to the pupils who will then carry out a number of tasks involving language either individually or in groups. A great deal of talk is always going on in the classroom—on entering an English room when a good lesson is in progress one will hear animated conversations in groups directed to the task in hand, see a number of children sitting reading or writing, see others in small groups working at some drama work, and so on. It will only be on occasions when the teacher is reading a story or a poem to the class that the whole class will normally be engaged in the same activity at the same time.

It is always the case that effective teaching starts long before one gets into the classroom and the adequate preparation of projects in advance is one of the most important aspects of the teacher's task. In the classroom itself he should be free to go around looking at the work and encouraging pupils and carrying out the very necessary task of servicing the project with materials, books and so on.

Although a great deal of creative writing is achieved by the pupils, the end product to a project is by no means restricted to the written word. Pupils are encouraged to present their work on tape and also to venture into visual presentation and model making. The object is to make the English block a place of active education in which pupils are constantly engaged in a learning activity and to have its walls decorated with a constantly changing display of the work that the children have done. Showing what they have done is made a major incentive though not in a spirit of emulation. We have abandoned marks, class-lists and internal examinations as irrelevant to the kind of work and spirit that we are seeking to establish.

The writing that the children do will normally relate to the particular project on which they are engaged, although staff are also opportunist in seizing on weather conditions, news items and such things as can provide material for writing activities. A great deal of free verse is written and we have some evidence that writing this in the early years in the school improves the quality of the written prose later on: at the initial stages the children will not make any conscious distinction between one written form and another but will create a form appropriate to what they are seeking to express. One of the most important things the department does is to produce a three-weekly duplicated magazine of about 20 quarto pages (sold for 3p) called *Inky Blots*, which is an anthology of the work done by children during the three-week period. There is never any shortage of material for this and it is generally possible to include in it work by children covering the whole range of ability, although excellence of its kind is the only editorial criterion for inclusion. This is read avidly by the pupils and an edition is generally sold out within a few hours of being produced and is in itself an important literary experience for many of the pupils.

The school's pattern of organization means that the potential fourth-year leavers are grouped together for their teaching and cannot, in consequence, be assimilated into the normal English mixed-ability setting. Partly because there was a need for it in any case, and partly to give an added incentive to these generally least-motivated pupils we began two years ago a weekly school newspaper which is edited by groups of these potential leavers. This continued successfully throughout the first year and has now become an institution which, apart from keeping pupils in touch with what is going on in the very large and widely scattered community that composes Churchfields, has come to provide a genuine forum for discussion. In view of its editorship the influence of this duplicated news-sheet is quite remarkable: the headmaster is frequently interviewed and so has been the director of education on occasion, and the 'letters to the editor' column provides a much needed opportunity for pupils to air their opinions, suggestions and grumbles.

Although we are very conscious of the need for a literary basis to the curriculum the amount of reading done by the pupils gives us cause for concern. The policy we have adopted of buying paperbacks is helping a little in this respect, but there is a great need for the provision of more material for private reading by pupils. Project instruction sheets always say 'You may read a book in any English lesson' and a fair quantity of reading in the classroom does take place. 'Block loans' of books from the library can also be arranged by English teachers in connection with specific projects and this proves valuable as many of the children find the library itself rather a forbidding place. It remains true, however, that too many of the children have not the inclination, encouragement or even opportunity to read extensively at home and there is a real need to achieve more than we do at present to foster the love of reading amongst pupils. Meanwhile a good deal of valuable work is done by teachers reading aloud to pupils.

Drama is an intrinsic part of the course although not regarded as something separable from the rest of the English curriculum. Thus there are no specialist teachers of drama in the school and all members of the department are encouraged to make use of dramatic methods as part of their teaching technique. Children will go off in small groups to try something out or to rehearse a piece of improvised drama and this is often used as a lead into writing activity of various kinds. It is very rarely that a piece of drama will be 'polished' for presentation to the class as a whole. A great deal of modern drama is used in the fourth and fifth years and usually small groups of pupils will read or rehearse a text together. The whole training of the pupils from the first year onwards encourages them to work by themselves for their own benefit and they do not expect everything they do to be seen or marked by the teacher. This is just as well as the output is tremendous. This does not entail any consequent sacrifice of standards and a great deal of the polished drama work done through Theatre Workshop and the material published in *Inky Blots* is of a very high standard. I think that there is an unconscious distinction made by the pupils as well as the staff between work intended for public consumption and that which is private to the writer only. We would see copiousness as complementary to quality rather than see the two things as opposed to each other in any way.

Talk is, as has already been explained, a central activity in the English classroom. There is no attempt to bring in any conscious 'speech-training', which most of us would regard as undesirable, but a great number of the tasks assigned in a project involve cooperative talk between pupils and the making of tapes is of course a valuable activity in this respect. There is little in the way of formal 'oral English' lessons: we would not regard debates or class discussions as being of much value, for example, and would prefer the informal talk of two or three children engaged in some such activity as making a model of what they might imagine the future town centre to be like, to give a current example from one of my own classes.

There is little or nothing in the way of formal language instruction in the department and any lessons in grammar have been totally abandoned. Instruction in the 'correct' or accepted forms of language is given on an individual basis as the opportunity arises and most of the pupils seem to acquire reasonable expertise in this field during the four- or five-year course. It need hardly be said that there is no use at all of the formal language exercise of the traditional pattern.

The object is to make the English classroom into an active place in which all the pupils are engaged in doing things all the time. It should be a place buzzing with activity and extending outwards in all directions. It is indeed no uncommon thing to turn up at a classroom for a time-tabled lesson and to find no one there at all. Groups of children will often be scattered all over the block, in corners, in cubby-holes, in cloakrooms and the like, engaged in varying activities with the teacher moving round from group to group supervising and giving advice and encouragement. A great deal of encouragement, too, is given to the children to go out of school to explore the local environment and to talk to junior school children, people in the streets and so on. A portable tape-recorder will very often be taken on these occasions (or a ciné-camera) and the interviewers will afterwards write up their experiences or perhaps prepare a tape or film based upon them. It is a good thing that the departmental staff is basically young as there is no doubt that this kind of teaching imposes a considerable strain and effort and is much more exhausting than teaching in the traditional way.

It will be appreciated that most of the work that is done with classes tends to be project based and there is little point, in the view of teachers in the department, in dividing 'English' up into the practice of a number of different skills. Thus, although in planning the syllabus divisions have to be made, we would not wish to see these enshrined in our day-to-day practice in teaching. There are not therefore special periods designated as 'drama periods' or 'poetry periods' though in our planning we would try to ensure that each pupil has a wide range of English activity presented to him at each stage of the course. It has proved necessary therefore to devise a system of record-keeping which will ensure this in practice.

The problem that faces us at the moment in this respect is one of development and continuity. Teachers who have been persuaded to throw away the traditional 'course-book' may well feel that they need some sense of continuity to replace it; and even imaginative teachers who have no difficulty in finding plenty to occupy themselves in the classroom may well come up against the danger of too much repetition of work from year to year. The answer here seems to me to lie in a department policy of linking the kind of project studied with the development and maturation of the pupils: one would hope, too, to keep alive a sense of wonder much longer than is often the case. Thus a good deal of the work in the first two years will be based upon and grow out of folk lore and myth: the third year has been most successful when projects have been concerned with what may loosely be termed 'archetypal' themes (e.g. 'the sea', 'the supernatural', 'the West'); and in the fourth year the movement has been outward to themes that very often have a social basis (e.g. 'rogues and vagabonds', 'childhood', 'war') although here we are very conscious of the need to ensure that English teaching does not become a kind of general studies or current affairs. Thus although a book like *Reflections* might be used with some fourth-year classes we would be a little suspicious of too much in the nature of a sociological bias and would want to keep the literary and imaginative explorations of these themes well to the fore in the work that we are doing.

The department is currently thinking a good deal about the problem of continuity and is seeking to develop an English course that will have, for pupils as well as teachers, some sense of progression built into it. This seems particularly important since other subjects have a demonstrable progression built into them, for the most part, and the pupils seem at times a little at a loss at not discovering the same thing to be true of English.

I am very interested in the use of the so-called new media for teaching purposes, especially the use of film, although the problems of showing film at the school are considerable and the money available for film hire is very limited. As much as possible is done on a small budget, however; there seem two approaches to the use of film which are valid here. One is the use of film as a direct stimulus for written work and discussion in the same way as one might use a piece of music—here it is possible to make quite useful lessons out of material supplied free from commercial distributors (e.g. British Rail's *Snow*); the other is to attempt a serious study of film as a medium in the same way as one might study a novel. This is on the whole too academic a study to be of much use below sixth-form level. Feature film material will normally be used therefore as part of a more general thematic study—e.g. a group working on childhood as a theme might well see and discuss *Les Quatres Cents Coups* as part of their work—in which case their response to the film is likely to emerge out of discussion and possibly through drama, leading almost always to creative written work of their own. As in the case of everything else that we deal with, we would seek to integrate film teaching with the total syllabus rather than regard it as something separable to be treated in isolation. The same is true in general terms of the use of tape and radio and television—these things will be used when available and when appropriate to the general scheme of work being followed. Occasionally someone feels that it is time to do something about mass media and such things as advertising—on the whole, however, we have tended to leave this once fashionable aspect of English teaching on one side, feeling that our time is better spent in developing the imaginative side of the children's lives and sensibilities. With only five periods a week available to us it is important to decide where our priorities lie and we feel that it is in this sphere that the English Department can make its own special contribution.

Some use is made of B.B.C. broadcasts to schools, especially *Listening and Writing* and *Books, Plays, Poems*. The pamphlets that go with these broadcasts are bought and stored each year and make a very good supply of cheap and well-selected literary material that is particularly valuable with the less able sets. Where possible the policy, with the broadcasts, is to put these on tape so that they can be used when appropriate to the course that is being developed as a whole although the mechanical provisions for doing this tend to break down quite early each term. A full- (or even part-) time assistant (on the analogy of the laboratory assistants found in science departments) to do this kind of work and to duplicate materials seems to be something that would save a great deal of teacher time and frustration.

The school provides for the normal run of external examinations taken at the secondary level: A-level, O-level and C.S.E. Normally there will be 12 to 15 in each of the upper and lower sixth reading English as an A-level subject; it has been the policy to enter about 60 children a year for O-level language and literature—though in the future this will almost certainly be reduced to one set of about 30; and the remaining fifth-year pupils (at present about 100) are entered for C.S.E. The school takes the examination of the N.U.J.M.B. at O- and A-level (this was a matter of policy to ensure direct comparability of its results with that of neighbouring schools when it was founded) and the West Midlands Board C.S.E. examinations.

At one time it was intended to produce a Mode 3 syllabus for C.S.E. English and a number of meetings of interested department members were held in order to devise one. However the board requires two years' notice of such a syllabus and the originators of the scheme had left by the time it would have come into operation. The department has therefore decided to retain the Mode 1 syllabus that the board provides especially as 40 percent of the marks can now be obtained on the basis of course work in which the school has a completely free choice. This has been found to be quite liberating in practice and our approach to the syllabus this year has been one founded on themes with the pupils being offered a choice of the themes they wish to work on. All pupils taking C.S.E. are taught in sets of mixed ability within that range and will normally work with several teachers during the course, since this too is now being run on team lines, with teachers specializing in one or two of the themes. The course proper does not begin until the middle of the fourth year and in practice we have not found it prevents us from teaching as we want to although the poor quality of the language paper the board sets gives us some cause for concern.

C.S.E. teaching is on the whole popular with the department because of the freedom it provides, and the pupils also seem to be enjoying the course provided for them which is seen essentially as a contribution of the kind of work they have already been doing. It has certainly proved valuable as a stimulus leading to the reading of a great deal more serious literature than heretofore; at present it is no uncommon complaint in the staff-room that classes will insist on sitting and reading and the teacher becomes almost a nuisance to the children. The language paper and the oral test are taken very much in their stride except for providing the pupils with some last-minute practice in the specific techniques of the language paper (e.g. notemaking) and the bulk of the course is built around the folio of work that will be submitted to the examiners.

O-level is certainly not so liberating a course and it is on the whole not popular with those who have to teach it. If it were not for the considerable social pressures, especially those of employers, we would certainly abandon it altogether in favour of the much more liberal and educational C.S.E. course. However, the member of department currently teaching one of the O-level sets has been experimenting with a much more creative approach to teaching it. In view of the content of the average O-level syllabus, however, and the meagre choice which schools have in the selection of set books it is difficult to see how this course can ever be of real educational benefit or serve as an adequate climax to the course that we have developed earlier in the school. One of my own pupils, for example, has just, as part of his fourth-year course, completed reading Dostoevsky's *Crime and Punishment* with real enjoyment and understanding; he now, for O-level, will have to spend a year in the detailed study of William Golding's *Lord of the Flies*!

It must be taken as a demonstration of the success we have had in making English attractive as a subject up to the fifth year that so many children, relatively speaking, opt to do English as a sixth-form subject. It is generally necessary to warn them that it bears little resemblance to the kind of work that they have been doing in the fifth year in the O-level course, and I would certainly prefer prospective sixth-formers to have done a C.S.E. course in the fifth form.

Sixth-form work presents a special and difficult problem at present. Although there may be some contribution from the department to the work of the General Studies team that teaches the sixth form there is no General English in the sixth form as such. This is in many ways a pity. All those doing English as a sixth-form subject therefore are specialists who will normally follow the course to A-level. These pupils fall into two well-defined categories. There are those who require a two or three A-level qualification to go into banking, colleges of education, and the like; there are also those reading sixth-form English because of a genuine excitement in and enjoyment of the subject, some of whom (though by no means all) will go on to read the subject at university. There is no doubt whatsoever that the latter group will include many who are capable of working at a very advanced level indeed; the former group, equally, will include some for whom A-level in its current form is both too difficult in its academic demands and also totally unsuitable. The problem is to attempt to reconcile the needs of these two different groups, which can be very wide apart at the extremes.

With the current upper sixth we have to some extent departed from our normal non-streaming policy in that we have provided two courses and allowed them to opt, under guidance, for one or the other. The one course, for the 'high-flyers', has been highly demanding and the choice of books selected for detailed study has made few concessions. There is no doubt about the high standard of work achieved by many of the pupils in this group and their involvement at the deepest level in their work. The other group has followed a much easier course in terms both of the actual demands made upon them in essay work and also in the kind of books chosen for study. It is expected that this policy will prove fruitful in terms of examination results. On the other hand it must be admitted that the policy has had all the evil results that streaming will always produce and the less able group has certainly suffered a depressed effect. Getting them through A-level has become very much like getting people through O-level a few years back and the two teachers working with these groups note the total difference in involvement between them. It is unlikely therefore that we shall repeat this policy. With the current lower sixth, which is much smaller, we are trying a different policy, including the adoption of a tutorial system, and it seems as if this may suggest the lines that we should follow in the future.

It is hoped that it will be possible next academic year to time-table the upper and lower sixths at the same time for their English periods and to have them taught by a team of three English teachers, all time-tabled for English at the same time. This will make possible the adaptation of our team-teaching techniques to the sixth form and will also mean that we can develop a tutorially-based course for sixth-formers which will enable us to make special provision for the individual pupil and his needs without resorting to the practice of streaming that we have had to adopt this year.

In accordance with the general line of policy that has been employed in the department over the last few years we have abandoned internal examinations except in the fourth year where they are used to sort out the potential O-level set as part of the supporting evidence we have available to us. Our feeling otherwise is that internal examinations do positive harm in encouraging a spirit of emulation amongst the pupils and that the kind of English teaching in which we are engaged cannot really be tested by examinations anyway. Also since we are now set upon a definite non-streaming policy there is little point in examinations relating to promotions or demotions. In implementing the departmental policy of mixed ability the problem that arises is that it is not generally possible to reach a whole year at the same time across the whole ability range because of the insufficient number of specialist English teachers —a barrier somewhere within the setting is therefore generally necessary. However, we hope to be able to time-table odd-numbered sets and even-numbered sets together next year so that genuine mixed-ability setting will be possible throughout the school (apart from the Remedial Department) in English.

There is therefore no need now, in English at any rate, to make provision for transfer between streams—the aim is to keep the options open for all children as long as possible and the only vital decision to be made is the selection of the O-level candidates which takes place at the end of the fourth year. Nonetheless the position of a pupil in the 'general' setting is important for his whole academic future, and the Head of the English Department accordingly has to take an interest in this. The transfer of pupils between general sets is decided by consultation between the headmaster, housemasters and heads of departments at a mammoth 'setting meeting' held at the close of the summer term when the cases of individual pupils are considered in great detail and when the general pattern of the school's curriculum for the following academic year is discussed. Although there is a great effort made at this meeting not to neglect the interests of any individual pupil, one is forced (as always in any kind of streaming) to bear in mind the necessity of making numbers balance as between classes and some individual cases of injustice may arise. Moreover, it is not unusual for this meeting to last up to six or seven hours and fatigue is bound to affect decisions made towards the end of it. Individual departments which operate their own setting policy are not restricted by the decisions of this meeting.

Since the membership of the English Department has remained stable recently and since departmental policy is decided upon democratically by discussion within the department there is not a very serious problem of continuity. The majority of the department are working along similar lines now and there is more continuity both in the work and the approach to teaching than could be achieved within the confines of a printed syllabus. The 'team teaching' approach is the greatest factor making for unity here and also for continuity in the teaching that a pupil receives, even though he may be taught by a variety of different teachers in the course of a year. It also makes it possible to absorb absences on the part of staff without too seriously disturbing the progress of pupils, and frequently nowadays when a member of staff is absent—even for a considerable period of time—it is not necessary to ask for a 'relief teacher' to be sent over. At present the team system is being used with the third and fourth years but it will be extended next year to cover the third to sixth years inclusive. (Whether it should apply in the first and second years is at present being debated. The feeling is that probably it should not; that such young children need the sense of stability that is afforded by a conventional pupil–teacher relationship.)

The basic principle behind the team teaching is that each pupil is assigned to a tutor who is responsible for watching his individual progress and who will write reports on him at the end of the year. (These reports are based upon a continuous record card filled in by everyone teaching the child throughout the year.) The teachers engaged in teaching a particular year are regarded as a team meeting regularly, usually weekly, under a chairman (not necessarily the head of department) to plan their work on both a long-term and also a week-to-week basis. The pupils in the particular scheme will then all take part in a project at the same time, with various members of the team specializing in different aspects of the topic chosen—one member of staff taking a turn at directing and co-ordinating the work of the project as a whole. Pupils may then sometimes choose and sometimes be assigned by their tutors to work with an individual teacher, or on a particular aspect of the topic, and the length of time that they will spend in this particular pursuit will vary, depending upon its nature. The size of teaching groups is also infinitely flexible. Thus it is quite a common thing for one teacher to be working with a small group, say a dozen pupils, on some such activity as making a film, while another teacher will be working with an extra large group viewing a film, carrying out written work according to pre-prepared assignment cards.

At the end of each project the teachers who have taught an individual pupil report on his work and progress in writing to his tutor who completes his record card. This enables a check to be kept that all pupils receive a variety of experiences in the English lesson over the year's course. There is also at the end of each project, which usually lasts about four weeks, some kind of exhibition mounted of work done so that the pupils know what others have been engaged in doing and recognize the pattern that has underlain the project as a whole.

The tutorial period, held at least once a fortnight, is an integral part of the scheme. In this, tutorial groups (which are of course mixed-ability groups as are the teaching groups) meet together with their tutor and may discuss with each other what is going on in the different working groups, pupils may have individual consultations with tutors, books from the departmental library scheme may be exchanged and read, or the pupils may write up a running journal they keep of the work that they are engaged in doing. The written work that they do may be used for display purposes, published in *Inky Blots*, and/or retained in their files by the pupils themselves. There is an attempt at present to move away from the use of exercise books altogether in favour of loose-leaf folders, but this is partly frustrated by a continuous shortage of stationery materials of all kinds.

The C.S.E. team-teaching scheme is somewhat similar except that each member of the team specializes in a particular theme and sets his teaching room up as a base in which this topic can be studied. Pupils normally spend half a term in studying a particular topic and producing work for their course work folders; they will cover three topics and may then return to previous topics to do more (and one hopes more mature) work on them if they wish. The topics at present being taken by members of the team are: 'the colour problem', 'the family', 'love and friendship', 'work and leisure', 'war', 'rogues and vagabonds', 'crime and punishment', 'youth and old age'. In all cases we are very conscious of the necessity to prevent this becoming a social studies course and the literary experience is regarded as central to the approach to these topics. The aim is to establish a continuity of approach so that the pupil is led in through third-year team teaching (with such subjects as 'the sea', and 'the supernatural') to a study of C.S.E. type themes in the latter half of the fourth year.

The evidence so far is that pupils and teachers have benefited by the sense of working as part of a team in this way; all members of staff know very well far more pupils in a particular year than they would do by conventional teaching; there is a genuine cross-fertilization of ideas and experiences between pupils and teachers; and, from the head of department's point of view, the scheme has been an undoubted success in building up a corporate sense in the department. The discussion that has gone on as part of the team preparation and the vitality in the teaching that has resulted have left no doubt that this is the right way in which to run a department, and under this system problems of continuity virtually disappear. New members of the department can be at once assimilated into the team and learn the department's way of working, while also making at once their own contribution to the continuous discussion and debate; and students working in the department get a chance of working with and seeing a wide variety of teachers at work. Another not unimportant aspect of the scheme is that teachers now habitually leave their doors open and wander in and out of each other's classrooms. We are all used to watching each other at work and receiving the impact and stimulus of each other's ideas in consequence.

It must be emphasized that the process of discussion is essential to the successful working of a scheme of this kind and that it is highly desirable that there should be built into the school time-table a period when all department members have a free period at the same time when team meetings take place —at present it entails the giving up of many lunch-hours. The scheme could not have been worked without the cooperation of the department as a whole and everyone participating has come to feel that the extra administrative work involved has been amply repaid by the new vitality that has resulted in all our teaching. I have described our team-teaching programme and the philosophy of English teaching that lies behind it, with a large number of actual programmes of work, in *Team Teaching and the Teaching of English* (Pergamon Press, 1970).

Little has been done in the way of specific preparation for the raising of the school-leaving age, although a committee of heads of departments has been meeting and trying to formulate a school policy for this. It looks rather as if what will be projected for the non-examination pupil will be an integrated General Studies course, run on team-teaching lines, which will seek to use the specialist knowledge of individual teachers while cutting across the conventional subject boundaries. We would feel that the English Department's experiments currently in C.S.E. teaching have a vital contribution to make here and would approach R.S.L.A. work in the humanities largely along the same lines, making as much use as possible of a variety of experiences, visual and aural as well as literary, with which to stimulate the pupils, evoking response in talk and writing. The aim, too, would be to make the course as outgoing as possible, with the pupils being encouraged to meet and talk to people working around them about the topics. Our experience in the department has been that, although these pupils are regarded by many teachers as 'difficult' when approached on conventional academic lines, they respond very well to more imaginative approaches to teaching, and, as always, the building up of friendly and cordial relationships between pupils and staff is fundamental to success.

Sixth-form minority studies are carried out under the direction of the Head of the History Department who is responsible for a General Studies team. The English Department as such makes no direct contribution here although a member of the English Department will normally be part of this team and it is hoped that some study of linguistics will be introduced here in the coming academic year. The need for a General English course in the sixth, conducted by a specialist teacher of literature and totally unrelated to examination requirements, is undeniable, but so far unobtainable because of staff limitations.

In sum, one can probably say of Churchfields that it has gone some way towards solving the problems of running an English Department in a very large school. To do this effectively a meaningful dialogue must be established within the department and all the teachers must feel that they are making some contribution to the formulation of departmental policy.

Adequate motivation is as important for teachers as it is for pupils if they are to be expected to do anything more than just earn their salary. In this department a great deal more is expected of them, including the expending of a great deal of time out of school in such unrewarding tasks as typing stencils for the weekly newspaper; that the staff of the department is prepared to commit itself loyally and whole-heartedly in this respect is one of the consequences of team teaching. It has already been stated that the syllabus is now out of date and will not be re-written; its purpose has been replaced by the weekly departmental meeting—a continuous seminar which provides the foundation for the department's policy and which ensures both continuity and consistency in its work.

The quality of the teaching can be judged more effectively by others than by those of us actually engaged in working in the department, but one of the things that pleases us most is the frequent comment from our many visitors that the children seem so frank, open and at ease with strangers. They are naturally friendly children but they live in an area which tends to be very restricted and which has grown in upon itself. For many of them a visit to Birmingham, only four and a half miles away, is a major adventure and undertaking. The development of fluency and ease of communication, spoken even more than written, seems to us one of our most important tasks, and one that we would claim to do successfully. Any success that we have is based upon the free atmosphere that we have managed to create within the English classrooms; good English teaching can never be achieved within an authoritarian system. The extent to which we have created a non-authoritarian system, with the pupils to a large extent programming their own work, is a measure of the particular values that the Churchfields English Department may possess.

Meaning in English at the Leeds Modern School

ROBERT SHAW

And now convinced at heart
How little that to which alone we give
The name of education hath to do
With real feeling and just sense...
[Wordsworth, *The Prelude*, Book XII (1805 ed.)]

THE SETTING

The Leeds Modern School is a local education authority grammar school for over 700 boys, of whom about 175 are in the sixth form. Between the wars it moved from the city centre to a pleasant residential area in the north-west of the city. It enjoys a good reputation in Leeds on account of its record of academic success, the contribution of generations of 'old boys' to public and municipal life, its 'tradition' (it was founded in the 1850s) and its location. It was established by prominent citizens, as an offshoot of the Mechanics' Institute movement, to provide secondary education for the sons of artisans, though, only a few decades after its foundation, a socially acute inspector was to complain that it was a predominantly middle-class institution, particularly favoured by the small businessman—a tendency to class-promotion by the school which was strengthened by the move out into the suburbs in the 1930s. Its curriculum was 'modern', in opposition to the classical bias of the traditional grammar schools in the neighbourhood. Thus it favoured modern subjects: English, History, Modern Languages, Mathematics and the Sciences, a curriculum for the needs of the continuing industrial and commercial revolution. Ultimately, the school passed to the local authority. Its present headmaster is a member of the Public Schools' Headmasters' Conference; at the same time, the school is about to become comprehensive—an illustration of that duality that has marked the school's history.

The catchment area comprises chiefly post-1945 and between-the-wars private housing developments, some now mellowed and green-fringed. The area is a 'good address'—from Headingley, now a little frayed, to Alwoodley and Adel. Green spaces abound. Industry is distant. The private homes provide Northern middle-class values of sobriety, thrift, tolerance (a little defensively), respect for competent authority and for a job that carries security and public esteem. These are, of course, traditional virtues inherited from Methodist practice and precept, making for reliability and honesty rather than adventurousness. Nevertheless, the picture is modified to some extent (though less than in the south of England) by the brasher and more recent ethos of a highly competitive and consumer-conscious society, and in the sons a reaction against the limits of materialism, in the form of political consciousness or underground 'pop' culture. The traditional picture, however, remains in outline. The school also serves a number of fairly small, attractively planned council estates. Whether it is the policy of the Housing Department to offer tenancies in this area only to 'socially desirable' and aspirant families I do not know, but the boys from these estates are not as a group distinguishable from middle-class pupils, either in attitude to school or in the values to which they appear to subscribe. There is one pre-war council estate, however, in the catchment area. This was part of a programme of slum-clearance from the crowded central districts, and the small number of boys entering the school from it has regularly included one or two of the most notable 'deviants' in the middle and upper forms.

It has been said (and it is not difficult to substantiate) that, while the boys in the school are not from the wealthiest families in the city (Roundhay would have that distinction), they are more representative of the professional groups in the city than those in other schools. A recent survey (rough and ready in some respects, but not altogether misleading) demonstrates the bias of the catchment area:

Distribution of fathers' occupations, Leeds Modern School pupils, March 1968, in percentage of year-group

	Prof.	Cler.	Skilled	Semi-skilled	Un-skilled
Form 1	45	10	39	4	2
2	41	13	37	7	2
3	41	9	37	9	4
4	35	12	38	13	2
5	28	15	43	11	3
6	44	10	38	8	0

One explanation offered for the increase in the number of boys from professional-class homes in recent years (compare form 5 with form 1) is the effect of the headmaster becoming a member of the Headmasters' Conference. This took place four years before the survey was made and may well have influenced professional parents in favour of Leeds Modern and away from local direct grant and independent schools.

Leeds offers the usual range of cultural activities to be found in a large provincial city. Although the region failed to support its professional symphony orchestra, the Yorkshire Symphony Orchestra, some years ago, Leeds is a fairly thriving musical centre with much amateur talent, and imports national orchestras for regular Saturday night concerts at the town hall, with large subsidies and low admission prices, especially for school children. A commercial theatre makes, occasional 'high-brow' offerings. The University Theatre Group's productions are well supported. The Civic Theatre has ambitious programmes by local dramatic societies, including Brecht, Livings, Pinter and Arden. Shortly, too, the Leeds Theatre Campaign will bring professional repertory theatre back to the city, without, one hopes, dashing the ardour and experimental zest of the amateur companies. Sixth-formers from the school, with members of the English Department, have played leading roles in the amateurs' productions and, recently, in the establishment of an arts lab. The local B.B.C. radio station has also been the scene of Leeds Modern contributions, including a controversial discussion on the teaching of Shakespeare between the headmaster, members of the English Department and sixth-formers.

Looked at from the viewpoint of West End or metropolitan cultural standards, of 'What's on in town tonight', Leeds can look very dead. A visiting lecturer from London, a Head of English in a large London comprehensive, was appalled, he told me, at the quietness of the city centre in the evenings. There seemed nothing to go out to. In fact, this paucity encourages the culturally-dedicated to create pockets of arts activity for themselves. The distance from London and from national celebrities gives local aspirants in the arts breathing-space to develop their talents. In this situation, the after-school arts activities of a school can readily interact with those of local societies and cultural institutions in the city. An informal Writers' Group, based on a duplicated magazine which sold copies outside the school as well as to the school, organized at the Swarthmore Education Centre a reading by Adrian Mitchell of his poems. The audience thus included members of classes at the centre as well as of the school-based group. The school Dramatic Society has produced plays at the Civic Theatre for this wider audience. The school has housed paintings, sculptures and architectural models of artists (and old boys) active in the city. Poems by the boys have been read on B.B.C. North. A member of the English Department has contributed poems to the B.B.C.'s regional arts programme, *The Northern Drift*; a sixth-former, to the local newspaper. In this way expressive activity in the upper forms can be related to the cultural life of the region or city and to tougher professional standards. It ceases to seem a self-indulgent, dilettante or merely academic act.

THE SCHOOL

The school is four-form entry. Boys gain admission on the results of the local authority 11+ examination. The forms are unstreamed and all follow a five-year course to G.C.E. O-level, before entrance to Arts or Science Sixth. Setting is restricted to one or two subjects—to allow for the introduction of Russian and to provide high-flyers in Maths. Formerly one top stream swept through to O-level in four years and there also existed two parallel bottom streams. Arts-subjects' staff were particularly unhappy about the immature first-year sixth produced by the high-flying form; most staff supported the headmaster's abolition of streaming.

Forms one to five are housed in the main school building, which dates back, with its uncompromising four-square classical revival in brick with stone facing, to the 1930s and its educational assumptions. The classrooms are fair-sized but too small for all but the most passive class-teaching lessons. Desks are arranged in rows. The sixth form had, until recently, been housed in a prefabricated structure, which had not worn well in its five or six years. The classrooms in this building are separated by thin partitions, which inhibit vigorous class discussion and regular use of radio or gramophone. A new sixth-form block, custom-built, has come into use in the last year, which provides more adventurous teaching-spaces, language laboratory and library facilities and social areas.

The English Department has no special drama room, but

we are fortunate enough to have the daily use of 'the scout-room', a fairly large room, unencumbered by desks and well away from other classrooms. Forms in the junior and middle school use it regularly, on an agreed time-table, to avoid the wasted journeys that 'on the spur of the moment' decisions would bring. Productions of the Dramatic Society take place in the assembly hall or at the Civic Theatre. We have a fair assemblage of lighting, set materials and good under-stage storage.

One cannot disengage a school from the system in which it operates. Its products will be 'used' in the economic and social roles for which society considers them qualified. In this sense, Leeds Modern belongs with the grammar school stereotype. What is marked, however, is the extent to which some of the grammar schools about to be 're-organized' have shown strong signs of attempting, in piecemeal fashion perhaps, to develop 'liberating and child-centred education', not geared to a technocratic scale of values. This may be the result of trying to redeem oneself under threat of death; it may be that, with their obsolescence, the social pressure is off the grammar schools—and on the comprehensives to 'produce the goods'; it may be that the staff of grammar schools are preparing themselves for the Day of the Comprehensive with an exaggerated respect for the egalitarian and child-centred claims (as separate from practice) of their colleagues in comprehensive schools. Nevertheless, despite their bearing the mark of Cain—11+ selection—many of these schools, in the last decade, have practised curriculum development and liberal teaching, of a kind and degree not generally acknowledged.

It is important to note this as part of the setting of our teaching of English at Leeds Modern, a setting whose parts—tradition, location, buildings, category of school, classroom practice—are often in conflict.

THE ENGLISH DEPARTMENT

The English Department consists of six teaching English full-time and one member of another department who teaches English to one or two forms. Opponents of the secondary school tradition of subject compartments and specialist teaching will deprecate 'inbreeding' of this kind. On the whole, I am sympathetic to their arguments, particularly when applied to the eleven to fourteen age-group, and in a system of teaching organized for inter-disciplinary enquiry, one would wish to staff along different lines. Nevertheless, within a specialist structure, there are advantages to creating a homogeneous department, in which the teachers have a responsibility to their subject and are not dissipating their talents and energies in attempting to teach a number of *specialist* subjects, of which English is only one. Indeed, in such a situation, it is usually English which suffers neglect; the other subjects can seem to demand much more attention from the teacher, in preparation and organization of materials, because they have much more subject matter. One is, moreover, only too familiar with the situation in those schools where the slogan 'Every teacher is a teacher of English' conceals a belief that the English periods can be taken by anyone, irrespective of lack of enthusiasm or knowledge. There is much to be gained—in morale, training and developing skills, sharing and pooling experience, from organizing sub-groups within the larger group that is the school staff. Within an inter-disciplinary teaching framework this will be a 'team' of teachers pooling skills in a cooperative project; within a specialist subject system it is the department which performs this function—and many a General Subjects teacher could substantiate the value of this unit, from which he tends to be excluded by varied virtues!

In a specialist subject-based system, it is even more important that the subject teacher should not be too narrow in his area of knowledge. Under inter-disciplinary enquiry systems the connections are 'built-in'; the various specialists cooperating have simply to contribute to a sum-total. On the other hand, where the subject is the unit on which teaching is based, where the total structure contains isolated units, the responsibility lies with the specialist subject teacher to suggest connections and inter-relations between his subject and other fields of study. The need for breadth is particularly urgent in a subject like English which embraces so much and yet has special claim to so little subject matter—and of this a university honours degree in English covers, at best, only a small part. One cannot expect omniscience but a knowledge of one or two fields or 'subjects' is a reasonable requirement. Along with breadth we still need depth, however, for the English teacher, for all the pervasiveness of his subject throughout the curriculum, is still exclusively entrusted with the formal study of language and literature and self-expression in the traditional literary forms. The specialist knowledge, skills and attitudes we associate with degree-level English are essential to much English teaching, even if the structure itself is to be inter-disciplinary. The best answer to these demands is either the *best* kind of specialist, intellectually curious and adventurous beyond his 'subject' frontiers, or the combined or general honours graduate whose degree has *included* English.

Other criteria to be considered in making appointments to the department are: personal qualities closely related to the role of the English teacher in the classroom, for example the ability to verbalize and the possession of critical and imaginative powers; evidence of genuine enthusiasm for the subject; ability to adapt to the varying demands of English teaching (literature, new media, improvised drama, language work—at all levels); special interests offered and the degree to which these duplicate, complement or extend the current range of specialisms.

It has been our policy to give each member of the department a full range of the teaching in the school, at all levels and in all areas of subject matter. Each English teacher has, thus, to be something of an all-rounder—or be willing to develop skills and interests beyond his own specialism. For this reason we have avoided appointments of specialist contributors of the kind found in many large comprehensive schools, for example, of 'speech and drama' or 'linguistics'. To separate functions is to harm English teaching, to break its essential unity of activities, to encourage highly formal teaching methods and to place the specialist contribution in an artificial context. There are in the department teachers with special knowledge of drama and linguistics, but they function as all-rounders whose specialized interests and advice are available to other members of the department. The exception to this practice is at sixth-form level, both English and General Studies work, where specialist teaching is given full rein.

Policy-making is the result of ideas circulating round the department. We enjoy the advantage of meeting at morning break, an occasion which is an opportunity for shared experience and comment. In a fairly small common room (by contrast with the far-flung empire of many comprehensive schools) contacts continue throughout the day. Formal meetings are thus not needed regularly, though assessment procedures involve sustained and formal discussion. In the day-to-day teaching of his class each member of the English Department has his own way, chooses his own books, and gives time to activities according to his own sense of priorities. 'The syllabus' which a newcomer receives is less a prescription, more an account of current, common practice in English in the school, its range of activities, the underlying assumptions, and the available stock and equipment. Few of the individuals engaged in English teaching adhere to tight schemes of work or 'programmes'. Lessons, however much prepared, are allowed to develop at the point of utterance; the responses of a class are allowed for; the English teacher may prepare his ideal lesson but once in motion the interaction between teacher, material and class or groups will dictate quite another pace, progression and direction—and set off possible approaches and kinds of work for the next week. The rigid preparation and adherence to preplanned 'responses' encouraged by many training institutions produce an undesirable 'sealing-off'—of teacher from the real and immediate reactions of his pupils, of pupil from material, of lesson from reality. A false sense of order results, a machine model of an impossibly tidy universe. In the last resort the process prevents that close relationship, the improvising insights, that we associate with English teaching at its most liberalizing. Lessons of this more spontaneous kind are apt to seem more untidy. They are, indeed, something like the dramatic 'happening', though this need not suggest lack of planning. Nevertheless, the teacher of this kind is less lazy than his too orderly and inflexible colleague. The nature of his task involves not only preparation but also (especially where a number of small groups are at work) flexibility, imagination, inventiveness, resourcefulness and quick reactions. Like Klee's paintings or Ionesco's plays or quantum theories, this approach to English teaching can look child's play (by contrast with sequential, linear, ordered models, where a false sense of order emerges from artificialities like 'plot'), but in fact it demands more by its insistence on allowing what is there—the feelings and individual responses present—to dictate form, than the more formal structured teaching with its pre-fabricated order, to be imposed by the will of the teacher. With the challenge to the primacy of the classroom as the chief location for 'instruction' and for the transmission of information, a challenge that arises from the new media of sound and sight performing tasks outside school that were once associated exclusively with print and the classroom, the function of the

English lesson in particular is becoming that of a 'social laboratory', a place and a time for developing the capacity for personal relationships and thought and feeling through activities of expression and communication.

SOME OBJECTIVES

With no tight syllabus giving uniformity to the efforts of English teachers at Leeds Modern one can only surmise the ends and objectives from the methods and curriculum—and the sum-total of these—practised in the department. By this process of induction the aims of English teaching in the school are:

(1) to encourage personal development and social competence through practising language in written and oral media in as wide a range of 'registers' as possible; (Since personal development and linguistic development are inextricably linked, the skills of communication will be taught more easily in this total context than in a narrower programme of 'Stick to the 3 Rs. We have no time for the frills.')

(2) to develop a critical awareness of the way language and other media of communication work, including advertising and the mass media;

(3) to provide opportunities for creative expression in both the new media and language;

(4) to provide a description of the English language;

(5) to develop an awareness of social and moral problems.

One could clearly develop each of these points at some length. Much will, however, be implicit in the descriptions of our practice. I shall, however, comment on one area of concern not touched on explicitly above, which is the class-culture context of what occurs in the English lesson.

The problem is one of providing through educational institutions for a common culture. Raymond Williams describes a crisis in English culture in the nineteenth century: 'Appearing in one form as the problem of the relation between "educated" and "customary" experience and language, in another form as the difficult relation between intense feeling and intellectual consciousness' (*Guardian*, 19 May 1967). E. P. Thompson, in *Education and Experience* (Leeds University Press, 1968), traces this cultural estrangement from earlier, the late eighteenth century. Certainly Wordsworth speaks for the emergent romantic movement, when he elevates the popular culture above the 'vulgar' (turning the tables!) values of polite, educated culture:

When I began to inquire,
To watch and question those I met, and held
Familiar talk with them, the lonely roads
Were schools to me in which I daily read
With most delight the passions of mankind,
There saw into the depths of human souls,
Souls that appear to have no depth at all
To vulgar eyes. And now convinced at heart
How little that to which alone we give
The name of education hath to do
With real feeling and just sense...

Blake sees the conflict in much the same terms, anticipating McLuhan in his insight into the role of print in narrowing the culture: 'I was in a Printing-House in Hell and saw the method in which knowledge is transmitted from generation to generation.' While Lawrence posed the separation:

'You know,' [Paul] said to his mother, 'I don't want to belong to the well-to-do middle class. I like my common people best. I belong to the common people.'

'But if anyone else said so, my son, wouldn't you be in a tear? *You* know you consider yourself equal to any gentleman.'

'In myself,' he answered, 'not in my class or my education or my manners. But in myself I am.'

'Very well, then. Then why talk about the common people?'

'Because—the difference between people isn't in their class, but in themselves. Only from the middle-class one gets ideas, and from the common people—life itself, warmth. You feel their hates and loves.' [*Sons and Lovers*]

Today, as Thompson observes, 'The educated culture is not encapsulated from the culture of the people in the old class-bound ways: but it is encapsulated nonetheless, within its own walls of intellectual esteem and spiritual pride.' This is particularly difficult to correct in a situation where education is an instrument of social mobility and a few kinds of intellectual expertise are commonly taken for a whole range of abilities.

Bernstein and Lawton make it clear, moreover, that new 'class-bound' forms may be discovered, arguing that the working-class child is linguistically disadvantaged in an educational system which communicates in the 'elaborated code', the language of ideas and educated middle-class homes, to the near exclusion of the 'restricted code' habitually used in the working-class home. McLuhan adds a further dimension to cultural divorce, when he attacks the domination of print-culture over the 'degraded' new media pervasive outside the educational system.

The question is one which will be solved in the total context of the educational system, as well as in individual schools' initiatives, but the English teacher, traditionally the high priest of culture and entrusted with a special responsibility for communications, has some duty to attempt to 'integrate' and to serve both sets of values, cultural patterns and languages. A modest start may be made by:

(1) introducing the new media of 'popular' culture into the classroom, not simply as audio-visual aids or in its artistically acceptable forms but in its representative examples, and developing not only understanding and discrimination but also creative expression in using these media;

(2) while, necessarily, having to develop command of ideas and 'elaborated code' language, maintaining opportunities for

'restricted code' work and personal imaginative work, 'the culture of the feelings' and the personal response *throughout* the secondary school stage;

(3) disabusing our colleagues of a belief that there is 'one culture' and making them aware of the implications of Bernstein's work in their own teaching.

Such concerns, it is hoped, find their 'objective correlative' in and give coherence to the otherwise isolated descriptions of practice that follow.

CURRICULUM

'I passed English all right,' I said, 'because I had all that Beowulf and Lord Randal My Son stuff when I was at Whooton School. I mean I didn't have to do any work in English at all, hardly, except write compositions once in a while.'

[J. D. Salinger, *Catcher in the Rye*]

If we substituted 'creative writing' for 'compositions', Holden Caulfield's confession from the American fifties could stand as an accurate indictment of much English teaching in this country today—in its unnaturally restricted and restrictive notion of the curriculum of English. There are, of course, historical reasons for this: the view that English was a weakling, unable to command respect (and inclusion in school curriculum) without the padding of grammatical study based on another language—Latin prevailed for much of this century, with a little bowdlerized Shakespeare and a few 'Essays by Modern Masters' (who were neither modern nor masters) added. Against this restriction the fifties and sixties reacted. Formal grammar in the schools was denigrated on the grounds that Latinate grammar is not a true description of our language, that its study was based on ignorance, pedantry and superstition, and that we learn to write by reading and writing and not by clause analysis. What was offered instead was literature. In the fifties, through the influential *Use of English* periodical and movement, itself derivative from the Cambridge criticism of the twenties and thirties, particularly F. R. Leavis, 'literature' meant a study of texts and of the contribution of form to meaning. Literature in this form could be justified in Arnoldian terms as a 'storehouse of recorded values', as transmitting moral values and as developing a critical sensibility which would reflect on and reform mass civilization. To this more recently has been added a view of literature in schools, less as a place for critical study, and more as a powerful stimulus for creative (imaginative) work by the children. (Sometimes this activity is also justified by reference to its 'curative' or therapeutic qualities, particularly in the work of David Holbrook.) Nevertheless, the tendency to underrate the work-capacity of English has remained with the shifts in emphasis from language study (of a kind) through literary study to creative work.

The shift can be seen as a success for the 'child-centred' movement which has characterized the best work of our primary schools in the last decade, a movement which has infiltrated the secondary curriculum. Its influence in English may be seen in 'topic' work; improvised group drama activities; creative writing; group- or individual-based work; and interdisciplinary arrangements. It represents a substantial victory over the power of the universities, particularly through G.C.E. examinations, to impose formal, subject-based study courses on the secondary school. In the defeat of a monopoly, of a bias, this is healthy. The activities listed above as originating in the primary school have relevance to the personal development of the secondary school child. Those formal studies which remain—from the university sector—also have a place in illuminating areas of knowledge for the intellectually able secondary child. Yet both are limited. It is possible that our need is for both—*and* more than their combined forces can provide. A genuine English curriculum for the secondary-school child would offer more than a preparation for the 'academic disciplines' of higher education and more than a development of the primary skills and work of personal fruition begun before eleven. It will also offer satisfaction of present needs, of those experienced at secondary-school age. These will include a study of the society into which the school-leaver will be initiated. This society can and is looked at in English lessons through reading and discussion of social issues described and enacted in contemporary writing. The English teacher also has a responsibility to help understanding of the cultural environment which is part of this society, the world of communications, the intrinsic qualities of each medium and how these affect content, for example. Faced with a cultural phenomenon of the magnitude of the mass media—and a frightening super-abundance is one of their qualities—the teen-ager needs help in coping with them. The world of the paper-back is one challenge here. It is not simply a question of instilling habits of discrimination—value judgements—or the ability to analyse components of form and content, as traditionally analysis has performed. The situation of super-abundance suggests rather an approach based on 'genre'[1] and on the kind of print medium a particular book represents—the possibilities and limits of that *kind* of book. One might suggest that to understand contemporary Africa, one might need to go further than the English teacher's traditional answer, a contemporary novel set in Africa, offering detailed enactment of personal relationships in a particular social context. One would need also non-literary works, like the U.N. *Year Book*, Luthuli, political and social commentary and works of history, economics and autobiography. Literature can offer what the non-literary cannot do, but it, too, has its limits.

[1] For the full development of this argument, see Austin Repath's invaluable article, 'Teaching English in a Post Literate Society', in *Screen Education*, 39 (May–June 1967), published by the Society for Education in Film and Television.

A secondary-school English curriculum, therefore, implies not only the formal and child-centred activities that characterize recent and present English teaching, but also a programme of teaching the contemporary social and cultural environment—of preparation for the social issues and communications-flood that face the school-leaver, through extensive experience of many media of communication, including the various kinds within the medium of print. (This last conflicts with the restrictive diet of books and close analysis of form and content characteristic of G.C.E. and the universities.) The result of such integration and development of English curriculum would be, at last, a full day's work for English—a range of activities, encompassing expression and communication, and teaching our culture, and for the secondary-school child, whether school-leaver or Oxbridge aspirant, a balanced and meaningful education.

Working as recently as 1964 with a belief in the centrality of literature, the momentum of our efforts since has been towards a radical re-orientation in our curriculum, of trying to 'put Humpty-Dumpty together again'. On the other hand, literature and creative expression will be retained in any responsible English programme for their peculiar relationship with the feelings and engagement with experience. This is particularly important in the grammar school, where intellectual forcing is common (and 'progressive' curriculum reform, for example language-laboratory work in the modern languages, may intensify it) and the literary and creative components have unique value in the curriculum.

TALKING

We are careful to avoid 'set' lessons for this activity—either of the formal 'speech' kind or of the less formal. We see talking, writing, reading, as inter-related activities, and not separable from questions of content. We have found the B.B.C. broadcasts in the 'Speak' series constricting in their separation of the speech activity from a total situation. There is nothing less likely to succeed than an approach based on 'How do we get them to talk?' What 'gets them to talk' is what produces meaningful writing and deeply-engaged reading: a topic of depth and urgency, related to the needs and experience of the group and a teacher who has developed a relationship of trust and meaning with that form. 'Talking' occurs in critical analysis, in improvised group drama, in film study, in preparation for a project, in group work on a film or sound-drama production and a host of other activities in English. There is no need to determine special speech or talking lessons, carefully structured, in order to cover the whole spectrum of 'registers'. This is not to imply that the teacher should not be aware of the linguistic demands and criteria of a situation in which the class is talking. This awareness is essential—and no amount of 'programming' will take its place. The ideal situation is one in which a linguistically aware and informed teacher is guiding talk, discussion or conversation on a topic or round content arrived at in the organic growth of the class's English lessons. The teacher must be careful to allow this development; often there is a tendency to overdo writing, feeling perhaps that talking is a waste of time. Many activities that take place in written composition would have been more fruitful in talk. The early school-leaver is destined for a life in which it is more important for him to be able to communicate fluently and express himself in speech than writing. The 'academic' child needs written competence rather more, but not at the expense, as it is too often, of oral fluency. And all adolescents have a need to share in the peer-group experience through the immediacy and direct personal involvement of speech.

WRITING

We aim to encourage confidence, engagement and enjoyment first in the early years, with increasing emphasis on accuracy of communication later. Thus in the junior forms the criteria are originality, vigour, honesty and verve—and then mechanical accuracy. The first priority is a writing situation and topic in which the child cares about what he is doing. Given this meaningful context, we believe, he will want to communicate—and correct errors. Our marking is intended to encourage as well as correct. Grammatical points, spelling and punctuation are taught exclusively in the context of the written work. Course-books and collections of passages for 'comprehension' and grammatical analysis are not used in the school. In the junior forms the emphasis is heavily on personal modes of writing—imaginative and descriptive work, in prose and poetry. Our experience is (and the London University Institute of Education survey into children's writing by Martin, Britton and Rosen so far confirms this) that the impersonal modes cannot be achieved until much later in the secondary school. Even then there may be discrepancies between a child's performance in one mode and his achievement in another mode of expression. Stimuli in the junior and middle forms include B.B.C. *Listening and Writing* broadcasts, paintings (usually expressionist or surrealist), sculpture, sound-collage on tape, film, television and the printed page. We attempt to encourage awareness of the 'conventions' of syntax, stanza and pattern by using work of a challenging kind, for example, poems by E. E. Cummings, William Carlos Williams and Lallans,[1] poetry by Hugh MacDiarmid, to suggest the effect of stops and words not noticed in more ordinary-seeming work. Concrete poetry and collages are also introduced, to draw attention

[1] Showing that the Lallans is not an archaic eccentricity but, like all languages, a special way of thinking and feeling.

to the visual qualities of typography, including spaces and colours.

In the senior forms the personal and 'play' elements remain but the range of writing activities is now extended to include formal and impersonal modes, including direct literary criticism. Nevertheless, within the topic-project, which will engage the class in class-learning as well as project group or individual work, there is always a choice of written response for the pupil: formal, informal, personal, impersonal, prose or verse. The only criterion is that of his feelings and ideas determining the shape or form or mode of his saying and writing. An imaginative piece of writing may still exhibit a critical response to the work read. Alternatively, an imaginative work of fiction may lead to a piece of writing of a formal kind—literary criticism, argumentative prose or political analysis. In his five years to O-level a pupil will normally practise, self-regulating, a very wide range of writing activities. A project on 'isolated man', taking in *Robinson Crusoe* and *Pincher Martin*, may take the form of a novel or short story or sociological treatise or literary critical study, or a study of the same subject being treated in another medium; for example, the work of the painter Francis Bacon, the subject of a recent fifth-form study. The titles are our pupils'; the choice of reading is their own, directed by the English teacher to relevant works in the form paperback library, a collection of Penguins and Pelicans, or the school or city library.

One must guard, however, against the use of a literary work in a project simply to 'tell about' the topic theme. A college of education I once visited had a project for its students, interdisciplinary, on 'water'. Students were to read *Pincher Martin* to find out about water—despite energetic opposition from the English Department! Clearly there is a danger that the literary work will simply be pumped dry of 'topic-orientated' material. At Leeds Modern we have always tried to counteract this by giving opportunity for critical analysis of work used in a project as well as discussing the literary 'medium', in relation to the work.

READING

Reading aloud is of value at all levels of the secondary school. A lively and sensitive rendering will bring a passage or poem or speech to life and meaning and here the example of the teacher himself and the standard he sets will be of great importance. This is, of course, no justification for those dreary routine 'reading round the class' lessons. The teacher will instead select and vary context for reading aloud: much more opportunity could be given for bursts of 'silent' reading. In the junior forms reading aloud has other justifications in addition to the literary or dramatic. Below the top streams of the grammar school one cannot assume that the process of learning to read has been mastered by the child leaving the primary school. The teacher can keep a check on progress and help to develop individual capacities by hearing reading efforts regularly—not, unless remedial work with individuals is necessary, in special reading lessons but in the normal English lesson on a poem or play or reader. Here the unity—mechanics of reading, understanding and interpretation—can be maintained, but, whatever the teacher's concern or intention in the reading lesson—mechanics or dramatization or both, we try to maintain variety and interest. Too often in the old 'reading round the class' lessons, whatever the teacher's concern, motivation is so dulled that little will be achieved.

Close critical study of content, structure, the contribution of form to meaning, tone, feeling, diction and rhythm, what one might call 'low-gear' critical study, are practised, but not as the staple diet of the English lesson. There are books and works of literature at all levels which demand elucidation of this kind, but fewer than one would suppose from current practice in schools! Consider the annual book-a-term term 1, year 1, rape of '*The Lost World*'. After two days, three-quarters of the class has read it, but spends the remainder of term studying it in class, reading it over for prep and writing about it twice-weekly. I am uncertain whether this is a distant folk-memory of Caxton and a period in our history when books were in short supply and expensive and the master read out from the sole copy, or later of Scrooge-like days, before cheap paper-backs were available, but the works themselves studied in this manner hardly justify such attention, which may discourage the younger reader!

Department practice has been away from this 'book-a-term' mentality. The need to offer wide reading experience in an age of print abundance and to make an outline study of the various media in print communication has been referred to earlier.

Projects offer opportunities for extensive reading, but books are also available for reading outside this context. Each form has one or two periods in a week in which it may read 'silently', the books being borrowed from the English Department stock-cupboards, which are unlocked and in the main corridors. A stock-list is available in each form. When books are borrowed in a piecemeal fashion like this, sets are depleted until books are handed in at the end of term. This drawback matters less, in fact, in a situation where few forms are following 'book-a-term' collective reading programmes. Extensive reading of this kind, for pleasure, produces strong reading habits and sharper written work. In the upper middle school the medium of the paperback is introduced with paperback libraries. These consist of ones, twos and threes of a number of titles, fiction and non-fiction, likely to be used in projects or simply as a continuation of extensive reading. (At another school where I taught, Woodlands Comprehensive, Coventry, boys bought and pooled paperbacks.)

There is even greater need for this experience of extensive and private reading today, when teachers can rely less on reading in the home. In an age of 'togetherness' it also offers uncommon opportunity for being alone—even in a classroom with others.

NEW MEDIA

Work in this field takes a number of forms:

(*a*) *Criticism of the mass media*—chiefly *content-analysis* aimed at rendering harmless 'fall-out' from the distortions of the mass media—in advertising and reportage. The work of Raymond Williams, *Communications*, and Vance Packard, *The Hidden Persuaders*, is helpful here.

(*b*) *Analysis of the intrinsic qualities, potential and limitations of each mass medium*, following the work of McLuhan, *Understanding Media*, and Russell Taylor, *Anatomy of a TV Play*. The contribution of form to meaning is central here. British Film Institute study kits are helpful. Representative examples are rather more to the purpose than necessarily good (art) offerings, though the study of film as art, for example, clearly has a place.

(*c*) *Creative work by pupils in new media*, at present at the pilot stage and a little limited by equipment available. With film 8 mm. is the main medium available but this has its advantages. It is cheaper and, therefore, better for experimental work, and it is less of a temptation to produce formal, feature-film work. Still as well as movie work is used. Our aim is not to produce group films imitative of the commercial feature film; rather a film equivalent of the personal writing done in school. Ideally, each child would have, for his film project, a cheap camera, with which he could 'get his angle' on the world around him. Work in the sixth form, as an alternative to other group activities within the General Studies set, is more consciously experimental: for example, emulating the Beatles' *Magical Mystery Tour*, which was not too technically ambitious to prevent emulation. Tape-recording is the other main medium of work in this field. This again avoids the formal and literal qualities that marked much English lesson activity of a few years ago, for example the senseless recording of work written to be read rather than spoken. Pirate radio station, interviews, sound-collage, radio plays and ambitious group sound drama improvisations, derivative from John Cage rather than Pinter—these may indicate the possible range of such work.

DRAMA

Forms 1 *and* 2

'Improvised group drama' activities, the groups selected by socio-metric tests. These groups choose their own material (often from work read in class) and develop their pieces over a number of periods before performing for the rest, whose criticism is generally fair and appreciative. It is sometimes more satisfactory to give one week in four over entirely to drama, than to break the continuity with a single period a week.

From Form 3

Improvised group drama now gives way (but still occurs) to working from printed or written text, both Shakespeare and modern dramatists, for example, Pinter, Ionesco, Whiting, Arden, Brecht, Beckett, Simpson, Osborne, David Campton. The emphasis remains on the texts as theatre, and not simply as words on a page.

LANGUAGE

In the sixth form it has been our intention to introduce some formal language study, following linguistics and the broader approach of Randolph Quirk's *The Use of English*. Below the sixth, however, language teaching is through a study of words in action—in reading, and writing. There is little systematic teaching of formal grammar, while comprehension is practised in the context of reader, play and poem, and not through isolated passages taken from context. By this indirect method a sharp consciousness of language and its patterns is, nevertheless, achieved. More formal attempts at 'productive' and 'descriptive' (but not 'prescriptive') language teaching await the publication of schemes suited to junior forms and surveys like that of Professor Halliday at London University. In the meantime, it seems better to have no 'direct' teaching rather than false approaches deriving from Latin grammar.

ENGLISH AND OTHER SUBJECTS

One area of cooperation has been with the Chemistry Department, which has experienced difficulty in achieving effective impersonal scientific writing from first-formers. There are many difficulties here and no amount of tinkering from the English Department will remove the fact that a child of this age is not easily objective, the strangeness of scientific method apart. Indeed the more realistic assessment of child development represented by the new approaches to junior science may prove a more satisfactory answer to the language problem than efforts of this kind.

Results so far have been: (1) to impress on science colleagues the fact that many mechanical errors in expression derive from lack of understanding of the content rather than inability to master the form; (2) to provide a more realistic and modest picture of the degree to which one can expect eleven-year-olds to have command of the mechanics of expression; (3) to show the difficulty of the impersonal at this stage by offering examples of imaginative personal work by the same children; (4) to raise the level of linguistic awareness in the junior forms to some degree by class comparison of different registers and language functions, including 'voice'; (5) to improve a little the capacity to perform impersonal writing tasks of modest scope; (6) to make the English Department aware of the problems in language experienced in teaching situations outside the English lesson and of the contribution English can make towards some solutions.

The time-table and the lack of availability of teachers from different subjects at the required times provide real barriers to inter-disciplinary work in a subject-based school, however willing and keen the staff to cooperate and to sacrifice valuable time for their subject. Some informal contact and help are the most one can hope for, though a proposed middle-school venture with the Geography Department (on underdeveloped countries, through factual and imaginative accounts) could be more sustained. The Music and Art Departments have provided materials and rooms for work in English relating to their fields, for example for 'concrete music' sections of improvised tape-recorded drama or for poster-poems, print-collage or art-poems.

SIXTH-FORM ENGLISH

The English Department contributes a number of options to the General Studies programme in the sixth form, including American literature, communications, language, twentieth-century European drama, philosophy of science, and expression in new media, the last a creative rather than a critical approach. (It should be noted that we offer no special preparation for the General Studies A-level or 'The Use of English' exam.) These courses are followed by mixed arts/science groups. There is a movement away from structured informational or critical courses towards creative projects and individual or group enquiry in a variety of media, including film and tape. This may be seen as a natural development from activities encouraged by the Northern Universities Joint Matriculation Board Project in the fifth form (see 'Assessment and examinations' below).

The A-level English course operates with two groups in each of the two years, followed by a third-year group of candidates for Oxford and Cambridge entrance and scholarships. This post-A-level group is often joined by interested and able boys in the second-year sixth. In the first term of the first year in the sixth boys follow an introductory course in English, designed to encourage wide reading and based on a critical project selected by individuals from lists of themes. These have included 'the outsider in literature', 'British drama today' and 'the literature of the two World Wars'. From the beginning of the second term in the sixth A-level texts are studied, with some provision for practical criticism of passages and poems and for imaginative writing. Opportunities for the last are much fewer than earlier in the school. Regrettably the A-level course, geared to literary criticism, meets the needs (and then chiefly the career needs) of only those boys intending to pursue a course of English study at university, that is to study a small area of 'English' deeply. It is a case of the universities prescribing specialization *within* the subject, at a stage when it would be fruitful to develop *secondary* curriculum and a wider context of study. It is ironical that the N.U.J.M.B. Project, to which I refer later, with its extensive curriculum and liberal approaches, including creative expression, attracts boys to English in the sixth form, just where it narrows into primarily literary criticism. This is complicated by class-factors. It is noticeable that many of the stragglers in the sixth are working-class boys who distinguished themselves in the personal and creative writing of the fifth but who are struggling to cope with concepts and 'elaborated code' communication. Indeed, the effect of the more searching critical techniques taught in the sixth (Empson, Leavis, Richards providing the method) is to segregate an elite who perform critical exercises of this kind with expertise. They shall inherit the earth—in English scholarship! But there are, of course, equally complex and sensitive ways of 'responding' which go unrewarded and little encouraged in A-level. (Creative work, for example, can be encouraged marginally in lessons and in after-school groups. The demand must be for its recognition in examination terms at A-level. It is significant that N.U.J.M.B. would not get away with Project 2 at A-level!)

English at A-level at Leeds Modern is arranged, for the most part, in double periods, the first period of each double bringing both groups (in the year) together to hear a lecture (possibly part of a series on a theme relating to A-level texts) by one of the three or four English teachers assigned to the two groups. After the lecture period the two groups split again for a tutorial or seminar, with one or two of the English teachers (present at the lecture). In this way the functions of information transmission and discussion are separated and more clearly defined. (A positive problem in sixth-form teaching is the uncertainty experienced by the class whether they are there to receive and make their own notes or to question and discuss. Ideally both should occur, but rarely, to judge from the comments of disappointed teachers on their return to the common room!) Another gain is the detailed preparation demanded of the teacher. The structure can, of course, be varied—to provide colloquium or symposium. Its application to General Studies has been delayed by the heavy demands it makes on staffing and also by the time-tabling of General Studies subjects separately or in groups.

ASSESSMENT AND EXAMINATIONS

(*a*) *Internal*

No numerical mark is put on a child's piece of work, for him to see. The English teacher has, nevertheless, to contribute marks for term orders, etc. The English marks required are produced by continuous assessment (the marks recorded in the teacher's book) with moderation of samples by an English teacher not responsible for any of the forms in that year. In this way some correlation between forms in a year-group is attained. Our objection to writing marks on exercise books is that they discourage the least competent and create an unhealthy preoccupation with competitive processes, rather than an enjoyment of variety. (Mark-flaunting by teachers can be a very cruel exercise; a fact which some teachers may have been too successful as children to appreciate or too hurt to want to reflect on! What possible encouragement is offered to a child who scales the heights from 3 to 4+, when he compares it with the 'worst' mark of the 'top' boys at 8? Further, the marks have dubious exactitude in real assessment terms.) The objection to examinations proceeds from a belief that in English we can 'examine' with accuracy only the marginal skills and these out of context. Continuous assessment allows for a wider range of activities and makes some attempt to evaluate ability in *each*.

(*b*) *External—N.U.J.M.B. Project 2*

In 1964 the headmaster of Leeds Modern, Mr Frank Holland, who had offered incisive criticisms of both weaknesses of assessment and curriculum effects in the G.C.E. O-level English language paper, was asked by the board to convene a meeting of schools around Leeds, whose heads and English departments might wish to take part in an experiment. The experiment aimed at finding alternatives to conventional examining of English Language and at developing curriculum with the freedom from formal examination pressures. The experiment has now spread beyond the original Leeds group; its duration has been extended and it is hoped to apply its method to other subjects at this level.

Within the space afforded here I cannot do more than summarize the method of working, the general implications and the practice at Leeds Modern itself. (Readers interested in a fuller account will find it in my 'Revolution from Above', *New Education* (Dec. 1967) or *Your Child and School* edited by Christopher Price, shortly to be published by Cornmarket Hutchinson.) The method is one of internal assessment by each school, externally moderated, through extensive 'blind' sampling (without knowledge of school grades) by an English teacher within the group of schools. Discrepancies, borderlines, and 'double-checks' are well provided for by second moderators, the supervisor (Alec Hewitt, who initiated the experiment from Durham University) and the final examiners' meetings. Throughout the year the English teachers meet to discuss policy and to undertake trial-markings. Correlation between school and moderator has been, almost without exception, good, and demonstrably better than the correlation between different examiners for the same paper of a conventional O-level English language examination, or between markers of different papers of the same examining board, or between the examiners of different examining boards. For statistical reasons it might prove necessary to introduce an examination paper. Results (i.e. order of merit, etc.) would still be based on continuous assessment, but standards between schools could be brought into line, through the yardstick of an end-of-the-year, unprepared-for test.

Such flat procedural description hardly does justice to the importance of such a flexible assessment scheme, for the results are not simply those of greater reliability of assessment. The flexibility of examining has allowed for freedom and enterprise in teaching too. No longer tempted simply to train pupils for the marginal skills traditionally examined (disturbing the lively teaching of the junior years), the teachers could re-examine fifth-year English work. The pattern that has emerged is: the abandonment of formal grammar and of formal comprehension and essay work; a widening of written activities, from creative writing to projects; increased oral discussion and individual or small group activities; a refusal to support any longer the separation of language activities from literature—many of the schools involved do not enter their pupils for O-level literature, preferring to develop literary studies in the 'English language' Project 2, alongside creative writing and practising written and oral language. In this the project tends to reflect the infiltration into an O-level context of the attitudes and approaches that have characterized much recent thinking about the teaching of English. What is new is not the activities but the fact that they can develop fully within O-level—and the children be given direct credit and full assessment value for their originality. In other directions the project might have been more adventurous in curriculum development, in allowing, for assessment purposes, oral activities (but not formal oral tests), including 'free' tape-recorded composition, and expression in media other than language, including film. The restriction lies in the label 'English Language' that adheres to the project. Like English teaching itself the project might carry more weight as 'Communications', an argument I have touched on earlier.

At Leeds Modern School the freedom from the shadow of O-level formality has been felt, as elsewhere. The project has allowed us the opportunity for *uninhibited* development (in the O year) of work begun in the junior forms—the development would have occurred (did occur) without Project 2, but with a little more restraint. An obvious advantage of the experiment has been its value as a training ground for younger members of the department, most of whom had to meet an experimental challenge in their first year of teaching, and as a place where we derived considerable first-hand experience of assessment procedure. This—and the development of our teaching, freed from restraint, at its most senior point—has 'fed back' into our mainstream teaching. The project also stimulated us to experiment in areas like creative expression in the new media which lie *outside* the 'assessment' pale!

AFTER-SCHOOL ACTIVITIES

Some of these have been touched on: the largely ephemeral writers' groups that occasionally take more formal shape and the periodical *Tag* which during its two and a half years sold over 600 copies three or four times a year, and the occasional connection with a wider cultural scene, either regional or national. This is a two-way process, bringing to the school in recent years readings by Geoffrey Hill, Jon Silkin and Adrian Mitchell. There is also the Dramatic Society (which in some years has a strong junior section). Provided the school play is not the only dramatic activity in a school, a glossy cultural-public-relations function, concealing the fact that drama is a poor relation educationally—and non-examinable, then there seems no good reason for the guilt about the school play that one finds among English teachers all too frequently today. We should, of course, provide for drama and the freer forms, but there must be a place too for the public enactment we associate with theatre. Much the same applies to Shakespeare as the school play. It can 'bring it to life' through performance—and for larger numbers than normal.

The Debating Society and school magazine are also traditionally the concern of the English Department, together with the dramatic productions that form part of the regular exchanges with schools in Marburg.

The most fruitful after-school activities, however, take place in the wider relationship, in the bringing home of significance and standards, through individuals or groups contributing to or receiving from the available cultures. Sometimes formal groupings, societies, having grown from past needs but now no longer answering them to the same degree, can take more energy to support than they justify. They may also, in their more vigorous expressions, provide contexts which are those of the coterie, sealed off, after school hours as during them, from the local community and other relationships.

CONCLUSION

Practice at Leeds Modern School will be different with each staff-change that takes place in a common policy-making situation. The practice that I have described arises from the response of a group of individuals towards a particular teaching problem—providing a total English programme in a Northern boys' grammar school whose tradition is academic and curriculum subject-divided. Some of the teaching responses will be attempts to correct the bias of the situation. Some, to develop the potential it offers. Nevertheless, it reflects experience less parochial, one hopes, than simply this. Educationally, it may be seen as the fruit of experience outside the 'academic tradition'; one would expect some of the practice here to travel well, for example to the unstreamed comprehensive. Culturally, the problem is one of transmitting educated culture, in a liberal and humane way, while not excluding the older experiential cultural tradition. In terms of method and curriculum this leads to a process of teaching which attempts to make a classroom a place which is a social laboratory, a workshop for relationships and expression as well as the location of 'instruction'—and to arrangements based on small groups and individual work. It seeks to offer the opportunity for learning and experiencing through a variety of media, and a range of language forms and registers, personal and impersonal. It is an attempt to combine critical awareness with emotional development, intellectual flexibility with personal integrity. The programme that will come nearest to achieving this is, of necessity, one of trial and error, of improvisations and reactions, which ultimately elude description.

Wordsworth, sentimentalizing to some degree, placed 'real feeling and just sense' in the old working-class experiential culture alone. We may find them more easily in a joining of the two cultural traditions, in intellect and feeling, through educational processes which derive their style and content from both.

Integrated teaching at Dane Court Technical High School for Girls, Broadstairs

IRENE SUMMERBELL

In *The Solid Mandala* by Patrick White, Arthur, the 'backward' twin, remarks to his clever brother: 'I never remember what I've been taught. I only remember what I've learnt.' If Arthur had attended a good primary school, where learning by experience prevailed, would he still have been considered slow and backward? Possibly he would not, until selection for secondary education came along and he was labelled so once more. At present, however, we are busy discarding the old labels—grammar, modern, technical high—and manufacturing new ones—junior high school, senior high school, middle school, upper school, comprehensive school, sixth-form college. No one can forecast what pattern will emerge, or indeed whether any one pattern should emerge. It would probably be safe, however, to make a few assumptions. Many teachers in the future will be members of a larger team. There will be increased resources, though perhaps never keeping pace with needs. There will be different demands upon the individual teacher. Classes will cover a wider ability range. Which brings us back to Arthur. We have to ask why he, and all the other Arthurs, apparently did not learn what he was taught. As teachers we are bound to begin by assuming an inadequacy in the teaching, either in content, method, or both.

In the Schools Council Examinations Bulletin No. 1 we read: '...a candidate will use his language well when he is involved in other subjects where, because he has something to say, and has been taught to say it well, he is unself-conscious about his linguistic behaviour'.

There are three important points here: having something to say; being involved; and being taught to say it well. Involvement, commitment, are especially important, but it is sometimes difficult for the teacher of English to accept the fact that the P.E. man, for instance, is not a near idiot because he seems to live for soccer and reads only war stories or spy thrillers. It might be better for us to remember that the grace and finesse of Stanley Matthews has inspired some decent verse. It is risky to assume that, in a group of girls who have watched with tense excitement a television version of Henry James's *The Turn of the Screw*, we have a captive audience for the detailed study of *Jane Eyre*. The boy or girl who is totally uninvolved in anything needs the help of a psychiatrist, among other things. It may well be that the teacher has failed to find the touch-point. Communication at any level cannot begin until contact has been made.

When this has happened, and not before, we can begin to help them to use language precisely, significantly, imaginatively. This will necessarily involve a teacher in numerous situations that are outside his experience. The teacher at times will be the pupil and there is no better way of identifying the weaknesses of his own methods. All the resources at our disposal must be brought into action. How many of us ever wander outside our own departments and share for a time in the magic of the laboratories, or touch the skilful shaping of materials in craft-rooms, workshops, domestic science rooms? Lack of time, or the alleged churlishness of colleagues, are not good enough excuses. The boys and girls in our schools are accustomed now to a degree of technical sophistication undreamed of by some of us. We must keep ourselves informed and use our aids—visual, aural and otherwise. We must use them, not they us, to achieve our goals. Otherwise, like Thom Gunn's ton-up boys, we will use what we imperfectly control:

> Men manufacture both machine and soul
> And use what they imperfectly control.

As teachers we may be wholly convinced of the relevance of what we teach, but unless we convince our pupils we are left with a roomful of Arthurs, who will reject what they are taught in school in favour of what they learn in the dance hall, the pub or the street. As a starting-point we must accept the validity of their experience and, through it, lead them to some awareness of its deeper implications, to the adoption of a scale of values that will not fail them. 'Matching our actions to our highest thoughts' has a smug, Victorian ring to it, out of keeping with the throwaway spirit of our time.

> Suffer us not to mock ourselves with falsehood
> Teach us to care and not to care
> Teach us to sit still...

The basic truths and falsehoods may be the same in any age but they exist in different guises. In an age, like our own, which excels in packaging, it is difficult to judge the quality of the contents. Yet, as teachers, this must be our main concern. We have to try to help the young people we serve to make qualitative judgements. If we do not make this effort we are not rendering them our proper service.

The inexperienced teacher is necessarily pre-occupied with 'What to teach?' His training will have given him some ideas on the 'How' which he may refer to, rather fitfully in his first years. He will also have given considerable time to considering 'Why'. He may, however, amid the pressures of a full timetable, marking, and trying to keep at least one pace ahead of his pupils, feel too beset to embark upon any thorough analysis of aims or purpose. Or it may seem that, having traversed that ground once, he feels he can now 'get on with the job'. In the classroom the youngster who continually asks 'Why?' is usually considered to possess a lively and enquiring mind. Yet we must be persistent questioners ourselves, of ourselves, because if we can achieve some approximate answers to this particular question we will surely discover that the answers to the other two come more easily. If a young teacher is confident that he knows why he is doing this or that in the classroom, he knows also what is to his purpose in the way of material, and the nature of the material will shape the method of presentation. Short-term answers will not do. It is no use saying 'I'm aiming at getting this group through this exam. This is the syllabus and we are working our way through it.' If the efficient dissemination of information on the part of the teacher and the gift of total recall on the part of the pupil are sufficient to gain the qualification, then the qualification is in itself worthless and we are not properly serving our pupils by involving them and ourselves in the exercise. If it is important, or necessary, to have some methods of assessment of performance then we must evolve methods that, while valid, do not inhibit good teaching.

The account of the course that follows, therefore, can be seen against the background of end-of-fifth-year examinations, with all that this implies in terms of pressures on pupils and staff, the demands of parents and prospective employers for qualifications. It is an attempt by a team of teachers, originally six in number, to participate with groups of fifteen- and sixteen-year-old girls in a number of different learning processes. The time, the circumstances, and the people most directly involved, have a bearing on the scope of the course, the aims and the teaching methods employed. The school concerned is selective but, on the whole, the intake is what has become known as 'the second creaming', the grammar school taking, apparently, the double-cream. The accuracy, or otherwise, of this terminology is not, in this context, as important as the extent to which it helps to shape the school's role. In this case, as in many others, it has meant the evolution of courses from the middle school upwards broadly based on vocational needs; a curriculum and time-table that give to the practical and craft subjects a place of at least equal importance to the so-called 'academic' subjects; the growth of a sixth form where pupils may be aiming at university, nursing, secretarial work, retail distribution, careers requiring anything from three to no A-levels. It has also meant, from time to time, resisting some external pressures to force into an academic mould pupils whose talents obviously lie elsewhere.

Part of the parents' anxiety that their children should achieve good examination qualifications springs from the knowledge that the school's locality offers very limited scope for employment or further training. The living is not rich and is largely seasonal. The population contains a higher proportion of the over-sixties than many areas. Prospects for the young are fairly thin, unless they leave home. When the school was opened in 1957 most parents were dazzled by its airy brightness and shining paint and pinned great hopes on what it could do for their children. Since the school is moderate in size, about 500, with just over two dozen staff, it has been possible, within the favourable climate of its early days, to build on and consolidate close parent–teacher–pupil relationships.

Establishing a new course, therefore, within this social framework had some of the aspects of a behaviour pattern within a family. The rest of the family may be simultaneously indulgent towards and suspicious of the 'break away' group. Some of their criticisms may grow out of anxiety for the welfare of the group. They are in fact proud of the talents of the individuals, optimistic about their grouped potential, but they want the rest of the world to see that their pride is justified. In planning the course, we decided to take advantage of the scope offered by the Mode 3 method of examining in the Certificate of Secondary Education. Our syllabus was accepted by the South-East Regional Examinations Board in the autumn of

1963. It was to be a two-year course, covering the fourth and fifth years, and the first group of candidates, 78 in number, would receive their final gradings in 1965.

In discussions which took place early in 1963 the team of staff who undertook to teach the course were, not surprisingly, agreed on a number of points:

(*a*) that existing examination syllabuses, in dividing knowledge into carefully calculated slices, not only omitted much that is important, but also tended to impose a fragmented outlook upon both teacher and pupil;

(*b*) that the fifteen- and sixteen-year-old regards much of the learning that he/she is required to do as unreal and divorced from life;

(*c*) that many of our sixteen-year-old leavers, even those who gained passes at O-level, are lamentably ill-equipped to face the world they enter after school;

(*d*) that a completely 'single subject' examination, at this stage, is educationally unsound.

The departments involved in the discussions on, and the shaping and teaching of the course, were English, History and Biology. Later comments have usually been that the first two are obvious but the third unusual. Recent exchanges of ideas on the place of the humanities in the curriculum seem to exclude any science subjects. This is a pity since it tends, if anything, to emphasize the largely false division between arts and science subjects. In any case Biology is surely one of the more obviously (to the pupil) 'social' sciences and, in a girls' school particularly, is the most popular. It seemed valid, therefore, to build on an existing interest on the part of pupils and staff. The course came to be called 'Twentieth-century Studies', which is comprehensive enough, and at least has the merit of indicating that the contents should be relevant to present place and time. When it comes to a study of literature with the young it is essential that it should be made so.

In considering practical and organizational problems of establishing the course, it is important to remember that those were very early days for the Certificate of Secondary Education. Regional boards had only just been formed and most were very involved in setting up the necessary machinery for examinations under Mode 1. We were naturally concerned to show that our course would be comparable with the Mode 1 examinations in depth, scope and demands made upon pupils. The syllabus was therefore set out in some detail. In fact this was a valuable exercise in work analysis for us.

In a 40-period week we could not allot more than 9 periods to the actual teaching. All fourth-year pupils were to follow the course and many had a fairly heavy commitment to G.C.E. subjects. The periods were blocked across the time-table so that a much more flexible use of time was possible, for talks, film-shows, visits and team-teaching methods where necessary. During all these periods the school library was made available for any one of the groups requiring to use it. In the first months of the course the historian, who was also school librarian, collected together in one book-stack most of the books on book lists prepared by the staff team and issued to each pupil under the heading 'Books for Studies' (see Appendix). This not only made some useful source-material readily available but helped to give the course a place of importance in the curriculum and to catch the interest of other staff and pupils. Many of the books had been newly ordered, with the course in mind, and so had the attractiveness of unthumbed pages and bright new jackets.

The next aspect of presenting this course for examination is perhaps less acceptable to educational idealists but was a practical way of solving a number of problems at that time. Obviously the pupils involved were going to spend a great deal of time, in addition to the nine periods on the time-table, on individual lines of enquiry, and in the shaping and presentation of material in various forms, written, visual, oral. We felt the course had to have more than one-subject value for examination purposes. The syllabus was therefore presented in three sub-sections: English, History, Social and Economic Biology. The third section caused some confusion, not only because of its rather cumbersome title, later reduced to Social Biology, but also because it was 'new'. No C.S.E. subject panel could identify it to their satisfaction and the board had to set up an ad hoc committee of cheerful volunteers to moderate it. The course is an integrated one by virtue of its unifying theme of man in his present environment. In general terms, we attempt to examine human beings as influenced by events, by their own and other people's actions; coming to terms, or otherwise, with their physical surroundings; as communicators, thinkers, creative artists. A *fully* integrated course on such a theme would need to be in the hands of a Bronowski. This is asking rather too much of any teacher. The strength of a team of teachers, each knowledgeable within a definable area, but sharing with the others common aims and a liberal-mind approach, lies in the contribution of particular disciplines within a general scheme. The course was accepted as a three-subject equivalent. The 'new' subject was accepted as educationally valid, and examinable. The staff were free to teach in the way that seemed to them desirable. An outline of the syllabus will give some idea of its scope.

PART I: ENGLISH

The growth of language. Emphasis on historical rather than purely linguistic aspects. The printing-press and its revolutionary impact.

Communicating. The recording of events from Anglo-Saxon chronicles to twentieth-century daily newspapers and including early poetic forms.

The dissemination of information—newspaper, text-books, public notices, road-signs, instructions, etc.

Communication in the more personal sense—novel, biography, poetry.
Drama and verse as oral activities.
The contribution of individuals to the community—the artist, writer, craftsman etc.

Use of language for work and leisure. Adaptation of style to purpose—exposition, description, argument, entertainment. The development of awareness and discrimination—the mass media and propaganda of all types, political, commercial etc.

The growth of understanding. Of individuals, groups, ideas and ideology.
A period reflected through its literature.

These groupings are obviously a false fragmentation of what must be in practice a holistic approach. The whole must be more than the sum of the parts so stated.

PART II: SOCIAL BIOLOGY

A. The Country we live in. (1) Welfare State: public services and hygienic principles as applied to food production, protection, sanitation, water supply etc.
Conditions in factories, shops, works canteens.
(2) Health Services—availability to all sections of community.
Public Health acts, the medical service, dental health, midwifery, clinics.
History, organization and equipment of hospitals.
Contributions of particular scientists—Pasteur, Simpson, Lister, Nightingale, Röntgen, the Curies, Fleming etc.

B. The world we live in. (1) Revolution in science and technology: development of nuclear physics and implications; peaceful uses of atomic power; medical techniques; agricultural improvements; harmful uses of atomic power; the atom bomb—its development and birth; hydrogen bomb; nuclear weapons.
(2) World problems of disease: bacteria, viruses, protozoa etc.
Social conditions leading to disease.

The fight: the body's defences; blood transfusion; immunity; inoculation; vaccination; antiseptics and disinfectants.

Use of insecticides on crops.

Men who fight disease. Anaesthetics, X-rays, radiography, radio-therapy, modern machines to aid surgery; use of drugs and their manufacture.

Personal responsibilities and the moral aspects.

The world-wide aspects—malaria and its eradication; work of Laveran, Manson, Ross, Grassi.

Undernourished peoples—fight against yaws, trachoma, sleeping sickness, leprosy, cholera, typhus.

The work of W.H.O. and UNICEF.

Diseases of the twentieth century, their control and prevention—heart diseases, T.B., cancer, effects of radiation, the physical and genetical effect.

PART III: HISTORY

A. The country we live in. How Britain is governed—local councils, Parliament, role of the civil service, local and parliamentary elections, rates and taxes.

Welfare State—health, housing, education, insurance.

Administration of the law.

Public corporations and nationalized industries.

Role of trade unions in modern industry.

The Press.

Architecture and town planning.

Work of individuals—Winston Churchill, Geraldine Cadbury, Baden-Powell, Ebenezer Howard, Beveridge, Rutherford, Fleming etc.

B. The world we live in. The revolution in communications, science and technology.

Causes of First World War.

The Russian Revolution and rise of Communism.

The League of Nations and its failure.

World depression and the rise of Nazism, Fascism.

The Second World War—U.N.O. Attempts at world control of disease, hunger, ignorance and poverty.

The Marshall Plan. The World Council of Churches.

The cold war—waning ideologies—U.S.A., U.S.S.R., China, Japan.
The growth of the European spirit—common market, E.F.T.A. etc.
The role of the British commonwealth in the modern world.
Problems of emergent nations.
Work of individuals—Hammarskjold, Nehru, Nkrumah, Verwoerd, Mao-Tse-tung, Woodrow Wilson, Krushchev etc.

The three parts are prefaced by a brief statement of common aims, which any teacher who sees himself as being concerned with the education of the whole person, can compose for himself. Details of the examination are not of primary importance here. It is sufficient to say that it consists of six written papers, varying in length from forty minutes to ninety minutes; an oral test; a special study on a topic selected by the pupil with, if necessary, staff guidance; and course work consisting of extended pieces of writing over the five terms of the course and integrating the three aspects of it. When it is remembered that all the examination papers are set, duplicated and, in the first instance, marked by the staff in school; that the oral test is taped; that the special study is retained for moderation, as is the course work, which by the end of the course amounts to five or six fairly bulky files for each pupil; then this appears not only a daunting task for staff and pupils but also unnecessarily complicated and cumbersome as a means of arriving at three final grades. The whole process could be simplified. It is doubtful, however, whether less than this, as evidence of the content of the course, would have been acceptable in 1963.

A summary of the impact of the course should show that, laborious though these methods of assessment appear, there have been, so far, no discernibly bad backwash effects on either staff or pupils. It is now proposed, however, to examine in some detail what all this has to do with the teaching of English.

In the three sections of this course, as set out, there is a false precision about the English. It is false because, in a sense, even after close examination it leaves us no nearer to knowing exactly what we are doing. Once a pupil joined one of the 'studies' groups halfway through the year; she enquired after no more than ten minutes, and in some exasperation, 'Well, what are we on about? What's this lesson then?' Another pupil in the first week of the course went home and told her parents, 'We aren't doing English in school this year.' Some attempt to illustrate 'what we are on about' will be made by extracting certain aspects of the course and showing, in particular, how these were dealt with during the periods when the English staff were with the groups.

During the first term the three fourth-year forms in the school look at the physical conditions of their own homes, at older or new houses in the district, new housing estates, Victorian terraced houses. They collect photographs of modern dwellings, well-planned and well-laid-out. They compare them with pictures of back-to-back 'two up and two down' houses in industrial areas. They learn something of the public services, visit a waterworks, attend a meeting of the local council. A local member of the council talks to the whole year-group on the work of the Urban District Council, local elections and so on. They talk to the local grocer in the small, neighbouring shop and compare his methods and conditions with those of the supermarket. They visit a factory and small groups visit some local primary and secondary schools in pairs, reporting back to the form on the conclusion of these latter visits. Factual accounts of the visits may be made (*a*) as an oral exercise; (*b*) in the form of a group folder which will contain visual material, (*c*) as an individual piece of writing.

In English the emphasis will shift from the factual to the human aspect. Houses are for people to live in; shops and factories where they work. There is a wealth of relevant reading here and the following are offered as tentative suggestions: 'Ally's New Year Resolution' from *Magnolia Buildings* by

Elizabeth Stucley; 'Memoirs' by Richard Hoggart; 'Going to the Fair' by Alan Sillitoe (all these are found in *Comprehension, Interpretation and Criticism*, edited G. R. Halson, Stage 3 (Longmans)); 'This Sea Town was my World' by Dylan Thomas (this is in *Things Being Various* by Simon Clements, John Dixon and Leslie Stratta, with photographs by Roger Mayne, the team who produced *Reflections*, a useful source-book of material).

For those who abhor books of extracts there is a collection of short stories which will have an impact on this particular age-group called *People Like Us*, edited by A. W. Rowe. A relevant story from this collection at this stage is 'You should have seen the mess' by Muriel Spark. This will perhaps have a more immediate appeal to girls than to boys. Examples of the way poetry can define and illuminate the children's experiences at this stage of their development might be John Walsh's 'Last Day of the Summer Term', or Edward Lucie-Smith's poignant 'The Lesson'.

Here is a summary of activities that formed part of this first term's work with the English staff.

(1) Individual written work in prose or verse (sometimes when prose is obviously more appropriate, guidance should be tactfully given. Girls particularly will attempt to treat all topics in verse):

(*a*) 'The house I live in'—an attempt to show how the personalities of members of the family are reflected in it and how far accommodation shapes routine etc.;

(*b*) describe a house (i) as an estate agent might, (ii) as it might appear to a prospective buyer;

(*c*) 'my early life'—the first chapters of your autobiography up to your present age (this was sparked off by Dylan Thomas and Richard Hoggart. Two weeks were assigned for the writing which in fact occupied about four);

(*d*) 'my father' (mother, brother, sister, aunt etc). Verse can be encouraged here;

(*e*) 'people at work': this can be an interview with father, mother or a friend of the family. Some chose to write it up, some to make notes and give a dramatized reading. A few taped the talk.

The most amusing accounts were 'My Gran in service as a girl' and 'My Mum's wartime job'—this was as a temporary butcher. But this was some years ago and, already, most of our teenagers' mothers are too young to have had a war-time job! It is dangerous to assume that what has proved stimulating and appropriate to a particular group will continue to be so for all time.

(2) Group activities; some oral:

(*a*) on the job—a taped discussion with a group of labourers on a building site. This was easy to arrange because the mother of one of the girls had already provided hot water for 'brewing up' on several occasions. So 'words had already been exchanged'. The girls involved—three of them—went around with a portable tape-recorder, owned by one of them, and dressed in school uniform which, they insisted, 'kept the language under control!';

(*b*) a display of photographs of housing in the area and some of the people who live in them with their brief comments;

(*c*) a report-back, to the group, of visits to schools in the area. It is important that they should be carefully briefed about attitude and helped to formulate specific questions, before making these visits;

(*d*) old people—a survey of conditions and facilities in the area. This involved talking to elderly neighbours and relatives, old age pensioners on holiday, visiting a number of old people's homes. They worked in groups of about four each pursuing a particular aspect of the topic, though not very rigidly—(i) housing conditions including old people's almshouses and homes, (ii) welfare facilities such as meals on wheels, home helps, medical care, income, (iii) recreational facilities available, (iv) the personal elements such as remaining family contacts, friends, problems of loneliness. All groups produced a folder containing their observations, some original creative writing, photographs. All held group discussions about their experiences, with the rest of the class listening in. One sharp lesson about method of approach was learnt on the very first day, when a member of a group returned, crestfallen, to report that her granny had told her that her income was 'none of your business thank you!' As a result of this particular activity many of the girls have kept in contact with individual old people, both in homes and in their own houses. They continue to visit them because, as they say, 'They don't really want you to do things or run errands. They just want somebody to talk to.' Of course, girls at least often have a much closer contact with grandparents than with parents. Talking to old people about the past gives social history a reality for the young. A pupil with a great-grandmother of nearly ninety who recalled her own grandparents vividly shared observations on conditions in the 1840s and in turn shared them with us. However inaccurate the old woman's memory may be on some points, the flavour is there as it can never be in a textbook.

Sir Edward Appleton once said, 'the communications scientist is not concerned with the human value of a message ...' But we must be concerned with truth and falsity and human values in communication. Otherwise, the dog's bark, the words (audible or not) of the latest 'pop' song, and an aria from *Don Giovanni* will be all the same—that is, nothing—to us. If as teachers of English our strong suit is to be communication we have to try to ensure that the message has indeed some human value.

(*e*) programmes on the theme of 'work and play'. Consideration of working-conditions and the contribution made by individuals to the community leads naturally to discussion of the use of leisure.

Each class of about 30 was divided into 5 or 6 groups. The groups undertook to produce a programme which would be recorded on tape. They sought out readings of prose and verse, and recorded in dramatized dialogue form 'on-the-spot' interviews. Some appropriate music was used and 'links' made, one member of the group usually being assigned the role of 'link' or 'continuity' and programme-producer. The exercise involves much reading to find material, writing up of discussions or 'live' interviews, preparing the script, rehearsing, polishing and timing of material and, finally, the entertainment of the whole class when the 'broadcast' is made. Here is an example of one such programme, excluding the 'link' material but including the actual items—(i) lead-in music of *Boys and Girls Come Out to Play* played on recorders by the pupils themselves; followed by a taped recording of a factory-siren, a pneumatic drill, typewriters clacking, (ii) two poems—'The Release' by W. W. Gibson and 'Work' by D. H. Lawrence, (iii) a dramatized reading of an interview with the youth employment officer with mother present (script by one of the group), (iv) two interviews taped at home with father (*a*) 'My job as a solicitor', (*b*) 'Down the mine', (v) a poem 'My Little Brother' by a fifteen-year-old girl:

My little brother plays like a puppy.
He rolls downstairs, off chairs,
Falls off walls.
But he never hurts himself.
My fat little brother is a jet,
A speedboat, a guided missile
Hurtling towards its target,
But never hurting itself.

He whizzes and whoos and clangs
And rides stallions and stormy seas,
Like Walter Mitty at the helm.
Then falls asleep behind Dad's chair.

(vi) hobbies—an extract read from a book on the subject followed by a 'talk' (after the manner of Joyce Grenfell), (vii) a group discussion on 'Automation and increased leisure', (viii) conclusion—'Toads' by Philip Larkin followed by 'play-out' on recorders *Boys and Girls*... Material included should be as varied as possible, involving much reading, talking, discussion, writing up of material collected, original writing etc. Other themes used successfully for programmes have been 'holidays', 'the sea' (both with a local application), 'old people', 'children', 'families', 'men at work', 'shopping', 'the fishermen', 'miners'.

(3) Reading.

(*a*) all pupils kept a reading diary of books, drawn from the duplicated lists at the beginning of the course. Talks and written work on any of the books listed were encouraged. Examples were: a reference book that was found to be helpful (a talk that attempted to indicate what we look for in a work of reference), a character (liked or disliked) from fiction, history or biography, an exciting episode (fiction or real-life adventure), a place I would like to visit (real or fictional), the most boring book I have ever read, two books I would recommend to my younger brother (sister, friend). Once a term they chose an interesting or exciting passage from a book they were reading, to read aloud to the rest of the class. Sometimes they chose to work in pairs for this and give a dramatized reading. Sometimes they chose to break off at the exciting point;

(*b*) biographies: in a course such as this, where knowledge and understanding of oneself and other people is the core, it is natural to encourage the reading of biographies. Unfortunately, too many biographies published for reading in school are either too slickly superficial or too tediously detailed in chronological facts. The biographies about the most famous are not necessarily the most interesting. George Hitchin's *Pit Yacker* gives more of the sense of the man, his time, and locality, than do many biographies of Winston Churchill, Florence Nightingale or even John F. Kennedy. Eve Curie's account of her mother is more vivid than the semi-fictionalized form of the same life.

During the first year, individuals, or pairs, chose one of the people they had learned about during the course and undertook to (i) read as much as possible, (ii) write up an account, (iii) deliver a 10- to 15-minute broadcast. This aim was to try to convey, not just what this human being had achieved but what he or she was like, to bring the individual to life for the audience. In giving an account of the life of Albert Schweitzer, for instance, the factual outline, delivered by one partner, was interwoven by quotations from his writings by the other. A similar pattern was adopted by two who chose to talk about Yehudi Menuhin and, in this instance, the talk began and ended with a recording of Menuhin playing;

(*c*) class reading: there is no justification for reading every word of a book with a class and few books, in any case, will stand up to this kind of scrutiny. But there are books through which the teacher will need to guide the pupils because, by doing so, he hopes to increase their depth of understanding, to lead them into an extension of their necessarily limited experience. In fact there are some works in particular which should only be read in this way with adolescents. During this course we probably read more poetry together than any other form because, as F. R. Leavis says, 'Poetry can communicate the actual quality of experience with a subtlety and precision unapproachable by any other means.' The reading of plays aloud is a curiously artificial activity at this level, even with one or two gifted readers in the class. Some of the plays of Wesker were successful, in the second year of the course, *Chicken Soup with Barley*, for instance. John Osborne's *Look Back in Anger* seemed to them to be about a world they couldn't even guess at. Some plays about the contemporary scene are as incomprehensible to them as many of the plays on B.B.C. television. The ideal is for them to see live plays performed in a theatre and to savour all the excitement of such an occasion. These outings are expensive, however, and some may not be able, or willing, to meet the cost, even of the inexpensive special performances for schools. If we really believe in drama as a means of self-expression as a way of giving shape to one's experience, then we will give it an important place in the teaching of English.

During the second year of the course we read *Animal Farm* and listened to a recording of *Julius Caesar* at the time when they were also learning about the Russian Revolution, the rise of Nazism, Fascism and the development of atomic power. Towards the end of the course we read *Lord of the Flies*. They enjoyed two novels by Nevil Shute, *Pied Piper* and *A Town Called Alice*, but these are for rapid reading, not detailed study. One successful activity with a particular class, in their fifth year, was the reading of the morality play *Everyman*. After this they divided up into five groups and attempted to write a 'modern morality play', with varying success. The attempt was valuable, however, in making them stand back and try to take a dispassionate look at the contemporary scene.

This account has, to a large extent, concentrated on the first stages of the course, getting it 'off the ground', though it has been necessary, here and there, to stray a little further to indicate how various aspects grew. It might be helpful to list several other activities which were developed during the first year of the course.

(*a*) The writing of travel brochures (mock serious) and the writing of 'guides to local beauty spots' (serious and as accurate and interesting as possible). Both of these can be illustrated with the cooperation of the Art Department and some posters can also be produced.

(*b*) The establishing of a 'talking-point' on the notice-board. Briefly, each week a small group, of two or three, is responsible for delving through newspapers and magazines and posting information, comment etc. on a selected topic in the news. This forms the basis for a class discussion during the week.

(*c*) A holiday magazine containing a variety of material such as stories, poems, informative articles etc. This can also be an oral activity and taped.

(*d*) The study of ballads and folk songs as they reflect the human situation. This can be extended to some study of blues. Most school anthologies contain ballads, the class may have what they call 'folk' songs and the teacher may have to produce the real thing. Here the Music Department can help and they may in fact want to do this part themselves.

Poems, anthologies, 'source books', records and films that the English teachers found useful during the course are listed in the Appendix. Deciding which set of poetry books to order is difficult when the money available is limited, and it requires much careful research on the part of the teacher to avoid too much overlap in the poems available in the anthologies in the English cupboard. But, whatever decision is made, some typing and duplicating of individual poems appropriate for one's purpose is inevitable. We run off twice as many copies as are needed at the time, preserve them for future use and keep an up-to-date record of what is available. It might help if a durably bound loose-leaf anthology could be produced where individual sheets could be discarded or inserted. A great poem may be a joy for ever but there is much competently written verse which may have impact and stimulus now, that, in five years' time, will have served its purpose. In any case, no class is quite the same two years running and no teacher can guarantee that last year's successes will be repeated. Some of the activities ensured that pupils did use the anthologies. In searching for poems on a particular theme they read many others. While not denying the value therefore of some recently published anthologies, where poems are grouped thematically, it might be as well to bear in mind that the search for material, verse, prose or visual, is in itself a valuable exercise.

We prefer to call the books of extracts listed 'source'- rather than 'course'-books. No book of extracts, however attractively produced, however lively in its contents, is the perfect answer for every teacher, the most appropriate material for every group of pupils. Some, however, are more useful than others and, again, many more of this kind are available now than when this course began. Most English departments will not be able to afford more than two or three sets. It is necessary to look at them all before deciding and even then one needs to make much use of the duplicating machine and photo-copier (the latter being an indispensable piece of equipment in any school). Not all teachers are competent typists and pressures on the school office are already great.

This is an appropriate point at which to stress the vital importance of the library as a centre of source material. Many schools are not within easy reach of good bookshops and, even when they are, it is not practicable for teachers to buy numerous single copies. So it is essential to examine a large number of inspection copies and for a group of teachers involved in the teaching of a course of this nature to undertake to read them. There is no quick way round this. Books cannot be recommended to the pupils unless they have been read or, in the case of works of reference, closely examined, by the teaching team. In addition to books, however, the library should build up a stock of useful source material from contemporary writing, newspapers, periodicals and magazines. The material has to be kept in some sort of order with a simple indexing system, otherwise much time is wasted thumbing through sheets and snippets. Small items are best mounted on card of quarto or foolscap size where a number of like extracts can perhaps go on one sheet. These can be stored in box-files. The task of sorting, discarding, keeping up-to-date is one for which a team of pupils can be trained. They enjoy the scissors-and-paste aspect of the work and will often be discovered lost in perusal of the material they are sorting.

At home attics, lofts and spare rooms are sometimes a mine of information on the past twenty or forty years. If there is no objection to the library's stock-room becoming rather like a junk-room at certain times, it may well be that out of the rubbish will emerge much useful source material: old newspapers, past copies of *Illustrated London News*, *Punch*, *John Bull* and *Tit-bits*. Old picture postcards are often a highly diverting find.

Some tape-recordings should also form part of the stock, not only taped broadcasts which will eventually be erased and replaced, but also taped examples of past 'programmes', discussions, conversations with parents, grandparents and various people outside school. Some of this material is more valuable than the history text-book because, to the pupil, it is more real.

One other aspect of the course should be emphasized before attempting to summarize what has been learned from this approach over the last five years. The pupils involved in this course have been those who are regarded as rather above average. It was right therefore to require from them a good deal of written work of a high standard. It is also fair to say, however, that all aspects of oral communication have been and are considered of the greatest importance and that, in class, more time has been devoted specifically to oral activities than is usual in the fourth and fifth year of pupils preparing for external examinations. With pupils of lesser ability, unburdened by the demands of examination syllabuses, oral work should take precedence over written work. All the oral activities referred to are suitable for a group of this kind.

The pupils doing this course had an oral examination, which was awarded 20 percent of the marks. Much of the course work, however, was the preparation for, or the summing-up of, an oral activity. It may perhaps be of interest to describe two of the experiments we made in examining spoken English.

(*a*) A week before the examination pupils were given three topics by the teacher to think about. At the time of the examination one of the topics was selected by the teacher and the pupil had to talk to the class on this subject for about five minutes. Brief notes were allowed. At the conclusion of the talk the speaker had to join in discussion with the class, answer questions, clarify certain points, defend a point of view.

This certainly avoided the prepared talk but imposed too great a burden of preparation on most pupils. So the following form was adopted.

(*b*) During the preceding two weeks each pupil chose a topic and submitted it to the teacher who could then give advice and guidance. The idea was to choose a 'talking-point' and try to express a point of view, rather than deliver an informative talk. Some had to be guided away from issues too complex or completely beyond their knowledge and experience. Some had to be discouraged from trivialities. They then searched for an appropriate reading-passage with which to preface the talk. This provided a test of reading, acted as a warming-up process and often gave a starting-point. The reading passage was limited to 200–300 words. Some chose verse and this introduced another factor, not easily resolved.

After the talk, again, the class joined in discussion and the speaker tried to defend or add to the point of view expressed.

The pupil's own choice of topic, with teacher-guidance, was the more successful method. It gave many a chance to mount a particular hobby-horse; it revealed, interestingly enough, that girls at least do not wish to discuss what adults see as specifically juvenile problems.

Finding an appropriate reading passage has been variously interesting, fascinating, frustrating and impossible. We consider it is still a useful exercise, however.

The class discussion is often in fact a group-discussion. Unless the teacher acts as a skilful, but unobtrusive, chairman the quiet remain dumb and the shy speaker retires and lets the talk flow around, past and above. They have to become accustomed to the situation over a long period of time. The class will assume the role of the teacher eventually, encouraging the reticent, quelling the bombastic. In time they will participate a group at a time. It is a fairly exacting process for all to engage in, say, four discussions in the course of an hour, or three in a forty-five-minute period. The optimum size for a group discussion seems to be between five and eight people.

I should like to sum up, briefly, the conclusions we have drawn from the teaching of this course.

For all the staff of a secondary school to work in isolation, strictly within their own departments, is a waste of the talent and resources at their disposal. It is not envisaged that all teachers should combine in a whole area of integrated studies running across the curriculum but there is a case for the close integration of part of the curriculum, specifically in the hands of a team of teachers who will necessarily, from time to time, seek the active cooperation and participation of their colleagues. The specialization of the individual has a great deal to contribute within the wider framework. In the teaching of this course we drew on the assistance of a number of other departments, Art, Music, Religious Knowledge, Physics, Chemistry, Geography. It happened that this particular team were drawn from the English, Biology and History Departments. Successful courses have been and are being taught in schools involving the teachers of Geography, Religious Knowledge, Craft and Domestic Subjects and so on. We would, however, always envisage that the English Department would play a vital role in such a course, in the shaping of material, in the sharpening of discrimination, in the opportunities afforded for self-expression and communication. It may mean that the subject called 'English' will not appear on the time-table in what will be for many the last year at school. The teaching of English, however, may have something to gain from this very factor.

The blocking of periods across the whole year-group means that three of the staff team are simultaneously involved in teaching aspects of the course. They may have ninety minutes or two hours at their disposal, half a morning or a whole afternoon. In practice this will enable the Biology teacher, for instance, to show a film to the whole year-group, with the other two staff present. A short preliminary session will be spent in underlining its relevance to the course and in suggesting some points to note and aspects to consider. The large unit then divides into approximately three groups of thirty for discussion. It might be an open class discussion or, on occasion, the class will subdivide into four smaller groups and then come together again after half-an-hour or forty-five minutes, however long seems to be required.

The History and English staff will learn something from the specialist knowledge of the Biologist. If a number of difficulties or areas of misunderstanding arise during subsequent discussion, it is possible to meet before the end of the allotted time, as a year group, for the Biologist to clarify, explain, answer questions from pupils and staff. The teacher loses nothing of value by being seen by the pupils in the role of the questioner and seeker after information. It should also be of some help to pupils to hear discussion on an adult level, provided the adults concerned do not always monopolize the proceedings.

Throughout, the three staff members will have been involved in the techniques of group discussion. In helping the garrulous to be coherent and the inarticulate to verbalize each will show a special concern for the use of language. To this extent each will be teaching English. This sharing of responsibility for developing the linguistic skills of pupils applies also in the supervision of written work.

The emphasis of the course is on human values. We respond to the human condition in a variety of ways. If a pupil chooses to write verse about poverty, disease, race-warfare, living in families, the Historian and the Biologist do not reject this as an invalid response. They will, however, try to make the pupil aware that this is one of a number of possible ways of looking at life and they will examine other kinds of writing with them. For convenience each pupil keeps a separate file for each of the three aspects of the course. An examination of the contents reveals quite clearly that they have been helped to write objectively, logically, appropriately, using correct terminology in a personal context. But any of the files might also contain photographs and drawings, verse, short original play-scripts, descriptions of an improvised scene, reports of visits, summaries of discussions. In exposing pupils to a variety of material—novels, plays, poetry, newspapers, biographies, original documents, films, recordings—the staff team attempt to demonstrate the validity of a variety of responses to a similar situation. Each member of staff is thus, at times, in a learning situation with the pupils. The course becomes a shared experience to which each department contributes its own expertise.

Because the beginning of such a course is so dependent on the team involved it is essential for them to lay down very specific lines of communication. Even in a school of moderate size, like this, it is not sufficient to rely on the departmental meeting or team discussion (and these must be regular, ideally once a week), or to think that it will be possible to remember what was said in the informal conversation during break. The work done, about to be done, successes, failures, must be recorded. Each must keep a very up-to-date 'work' book for his own perusal, so that he can share his ideas with the team in order that new staff can be fully briefed about what is going on. The success of the course depends on full documentation and, with this, will survive staff changes.

Demands on the teaching team are considerable in finding source material, duplicating, extending their own knowledge, since they must be at least in touch with what their colleagues are teaching. They need the support of the rest of the staff, considerable resources in the provision of books, tape-recorders, gramophones and a flexible time-table that will give blocks of time for the course and sufficient time to teach it. We had nine periods in a crowded time-table. We would have had less pressure with about twelve periods and, with pupils of less ability than ours, fifteen in a 40-period week would be more realistic.

Staff/pupil relationships gain from this approach to teaching. The teacher is himself often involved in a learning situation. It becomes a sharing of experience, albeit with the teacher often as the guide, as all are involved in the process of seeking for and adapting material to a particular purpose. The synthesis of knowledge comes naturally to the pupils; it is the school time-table (and those who teach it) which divides it up into convenient slices. It is stimulating for the pupils to see that the teacher has wider interests than his 'subject' hitherto implied. This is another reason why, at this level, we might lose nothing, and gain something, by dropping some familiar 'subjects' from the time-table. If the pupil feels he is doing something 'new', something which takes him often outside the confines of the school building, he may see his last year at school as something more than the tedious wait before he goes out into the 'real' world. We have found over the last five years that many of the pupils involved in this course are willing to devote a great deal of time out-of-school on group work, individual studies, special assignments, collection of material, discovery of sources, visits etc. The rest of the family, friends, other staff, have all been pressed into service in their researches. We have had heartfelt remarks from fathers that they would like to be able to see the daily paper in the evening before it took on the appearance of a lace doyley. In fact they have been willing to spend time on 'studies' to the detriment of other subjects though, in general, the impact of the course on other areas of the curriculum has been wholly good, in so far as they have been able to discern the relationship between one area of knowledge and another.

Even in a school such as this, where all pupils are considered selective material, there is a considerable variation in performance. These pupils, after all, are considered to be less 'academic' than their grammar-school counterparts. We have found that this course has had a considerable impact on their degree of fluency, both written and spoken. We have had a number of unsolicited testimonials from local employers that the fifth-year pupils seeking employment 'interview well'. It is not glibness that we wish to encourage in schools but a direct and honest contact with other human beings, a certain degree of self-confidence, the expectation of being listened to sympathetically, and the ability to use language competently. Perhaps one or two of the pupils can have the last word and we as teachers can learn something from what they say. These are all comments from fifteen-year-olds made during the first year of the course:

Time-tables are usually very unexciting as they have to be made up according to convenience rather than enjoyment.

A time-table is made up on the spur of the moment. The curriculum is for all time.

I like the teacher to teach us from her mind not from the book.

APPENDIX

I. BOOKS FOR 'TWENTIETH-CENTURY STUDIES'

[Each pupil has a personal copy of this list, with blank pages for additions and notes.]

General

From Magic to Medicine. R. Calder.
Science on the March: Health. John Clark.
Science and the Doctor. F. Elwell.
The Romance of Medicine. J. Hayward.
Mankind against the Killers. J. Hemming.
The Story of Hospital Almoners. E. M. Bell.
A Short History of Nursing. W. R. Bett.
The Nurse and her World. P. Bright.
The Story of Nursing. J. M. Calder.
The Story of St Thomas's. C. Graves.
Medicine. B. Taylor.
A Handbook of Hygiene and Health Education. C. Eastwood.
Health, Personal and Communal. J. Gibson.
Science and your Health. K. Kutchin.
The Life-Savers. R. Calder.
The World of the Infinitely Small. L. Ludovici.
A Short History of Medicine. F. Poynter.
Atoms and Energy. F. R. Elwell.
British Nuclear Reactors. G. Gibbons.
Prospects for Thermo-nuclear Power. T. F. Johns.
Atomic Energy. E. Lawsen.
The Atom: Friend or Foe? C. N. Martin.
The Microphysical World. W. Wilson.
Atoms at Work. J. Mander.
Inside the Atom. M. Neurath.
Electrons at Work. F. J. M. Laver.

Collected biographies

Pioneers of the Modern World. E. H. Carter.
They Fought for Children. P. Chambers.

Integrated teaching at Dane Court Technical High School

Break Through in Science. I. Asimov.
Six Great Scientists. J. G. Crowther.
British Scientists of the Twentieth Century. J. G. Crowther.
Men and Women behind the Atom. S. R. Reidman.
Living Names—Seven Biologists. T. H. Savory.
Great Biologists. H. Williams.
Modern Scientists at Work. N. Wymer.
Great Healers. K. Newstead Flint.
Great Discoveries in Modern Science. P. Pringle.
Masters of Medicine. H. Williams.
Between Life and Death. H. Williams.

Individual biographies

Sir Alexander Fleming. K. Surrey.
Florence Nightingale. L. Seymer.
Florence Nightingale. M. Leighton.
Florence Nightingale. E. White.
Louis Pasteur. A. S. Malkus.
Louis Pasteur. N. Pain.
Sir Ronald Ross: the Mosquito Man. J. Rowland.
Albert Schweitzer: All Men are Brothers. C. M. Simon.
Albert Schweitzer: the Story of his Life and Work. N. Langley.
The Story of Albert Schweitzer. Jo Manton.

Books about words

The Spell of Words. John & Joan Levitt.
The Tree of Language. Helen & Charlton Laird.
The 26 Letters. Oscar Ogg.
Mind Your Language. Ivor Brown.

Books about communicating

From Drum Beat to Tickertape. Edward Osmond.
Pages, Pictures and Print. Joanna Foster.
A Book is made for You. R. H. Havercroft.
Black on White. M. Uin.
The Story of the Book. Agnes Allen.
Newspapers. Henry Compton.
Advertising in Modern Life. John Cloag.

The Cinema. Stanley Reed.
What Shall I Say? Lola Mulcaster.
Looking Ahead. E. Johnson & C. G. Wilkinson.

Books about people

Family Life in Great Britain. P. Edwards-Rees.
The Good Citizen. C. S. Higham.
Are Findings Keepings? Claud Mullins.
Farthest North. F. Nansen.
The Story of My Life. Helen Keller.
Kagawa of Japan. C. J. Davey.
A Time From the World. Rowena Farre.
The Sixth Race. R. M. Bartlett.
Refugee World. Robert Kee.
Malaria Ross. Josephine Kamm.
Madame Curie. Eve Curie.
Six Against Tyranny. Inge Scholl.
The Wooden Horse. Eric Williams.
The People's Earl. M. St J. Fancourt.
The Small Woman. Alan Burgess.
Friend Within the Gates [Edith Cavell]. Elizabeth Grey.
The Autobiography of a Super Tramp. W. H. Davies.
Dag Hammarskjold. Sten Soderberg.
Rain and the Feast of Stars. Reiko Hatsumi.
Pit Yacker. George Hitchen.
President Kennedy. Frances Wilkins.
Nehru. Michael Edwardes.
Alfred Nobel. Erik Bergenson.
A Doctor Alone. Peggy Chambers.

Books about pleasure

Entertainment. John Kay.
Enjoying Paintings. A. C. Ward.
The Artist and His World. Julian Trevelyan.
Going to a Concert. Lionel Salter.
First Steps in Art Appreciation. Nika Hulton.
Going to the Theatre. John Allen.

Books for your leisure

Out of this World, Vol. I. A. C. Clarke.
Out of this World, Vol. II. J. M. White.
Aspects of Science Fiction. G. D. Doherty.
People and Diamonds, 1 & 2. David Holbrook.
Last Year's Broken Toys. Barbara Kerr-Wilson.
The Day Before Yesterday. Noel Streatfeild.
Mary Jane. Dorothy Sterling.
Out of Step. Josephine Kamm.
The Sea Broke Through. A. Flankaberg.
Devil's Hill. Nan Chauncey.
The Whinstone Drift. Richard Armstrong.
Lost in the Barrens. Farley Mowatt.
Sparks Among the Stubble. E. Vipont.
The Day of the Bomb. Karl Bruckner.
Flowers of Hiroshima. Edita Morris.
The Pit. Reginald Maddock.
The Crab-Apple Tree. Richard Church.
Pastures of the Blue Crane. H. F. Brinsmead.
Red Moon and High Summer. Herbert Kaufman.
Dandelion Wine. Ray Bradbury.
Grandad With Snails. Michael Baldwin.

II. POEMS, ANTHOLOGIES, 'SOURCE BOOKS', RECORDINGS, FILMS

[These were found especially useful by the English teachers during the course.]

Poems

'An Old Man's Hands'. Margaret Stanley-Wrench.
'My Grandmother'. Elizabeth Jennings.
'Prayer of a Black Boy'. Guy Tirolien.
'Suburban Dream'. Edwin Muir.
'Toads'. Philip Larkin.
'My Parents Kept me from Children who were Rough'. Stephen Spender.
'Song Before Breakfast'. Ogden Nash.

'Peekaboo I almost see you'. Ogden Nash.
'Tyne Dock'. Francis Scarfe.
'The War Against Trees'. Stanley Kunitz.
'She said—'. Walter de la Mare.
'The Man in the Bowler Hat'. A. S. J. Tessimond.
'The Songs'. Martin Bell.
'Your Attention Please'. Peter Porter.
'Defencc'. Jon Silkin.
'Race'. Karen Gershon.

[This group of poems can be found in the anthologies listed below.]

'Death of a Son'. Jon Silkin.
'The Rainwalker'. Denis Levertov.
'A Solitude'. Denis Levertov.
'A Figure of Time'. Denis Levertov.
'A Moment of Respect'. Edwin Brock.
'Only Child'. Edwin Brock.
'Timothy Winters'. Charles Causley.
'Old Woman'. Elizabeth Jennings.
'A Prospect of Children'. Laurence Durrell.
'An Old Man'. R. S. Thomas.
'Soil'. R. S. Thomas.
'My Friend Maloney'. Charles Causley.
'Five Ways to Kill a Man'. Edwin Brock.

[All these can be found in the Penguin 'Modern Poets' series.]

'Microcosm'. Richard Kell.
'Sea-captain'. Hal Summers.
'Remembering the War'. George MacBeth.
'Change of Season'. J. E. Weir.
'The Taxi-driver'. Patric Dickinson.
'Old Man'. Vernon Scannell.
'Lines to a Child'. J. E. Weir.
'The Nightmare'. Elizabeth Jennings.
'Stirrings'. I. H. Seed.

[These were broadcast in the Third Programme, and reprinted in *The Listener*.]

Integrated teaching at Dane Court Technical High School

Anthologies

This Day and Age. S. Hewitt (Ed. Arnold).
Every Man will Shout. R. Mansfield & L. Armstrong (Faber).
Feet on the Ground. M. J. O'Donnell (Blackie).
The Modern Poet's World. James Reeves (Heinemann).
Six Modern Poets. J. R. Osgerby (Chatto & Windus).
Happenings. R. Wollman & D. Grugeon (Harrap).
The Making of Man. R. B. Heath (Nelson).
Modern Poems Understood. C. W. Gillam (Harrap).
Flash Point. Robert Shaw (E. J. Arnold).
Poems of Our Time. (Everyman's Library).
The Harrap Book of Modern Verse. Wollman & Parker (Harrap).
You Come Too. Robert Frost (Bodley Head).

Source books

Reflections. Simon Clements, John Dixon, Leslie Stratta (teacher's book available; O.U.P.).
Things Being Various. Same team as above (O.U.P.). [This contains poems as well as prose and is more literary in content than the above.]

What's Your Opinion? Philip Grosset (Evans Bros).
Topics in English. Geoffrey Summerfield (Batsford).
Take a Look. G. Lawrence (Pergamon).
Useful Literacy.
Progressive Literacy.
Life & Literacy. [Emphasis on oral activities.]
} P. J. McGeeney (Cassell).

Recordings

Documentary records available from John Murray:
B.B.C. *Scrapbook for 1914.*
Scrapbook for 1940.
Scrapbook for 1945.
I Can Hear It Now. [Excerpts from speeches of Sir Winston Churchill.]

Folk songs etc. available from Topic Records Ltd., 27 Nassington Road, N.W.3.:

The Iron Muse (12T 86).

A collection of industrial folk songs:

Steam Whistle Ballads (12T 104).

Workers' songs of the nineteenth century:

Frost & Fire (12T 136).

Ceremonial folk songs:

Roll on Buddy (12T 105).
American folk songs

There are numerous other Topic recordings of folk song that have the vivid feeling and often racy flavour of a particular place and time. Comparing these recordings with many that pupils will be willing to provide can help to reveal the artificiality and spuriousness of much that is now erroneously described as 'folk' song.

Films

Full-length:

Twelve Angry Men (United Artists; 92 mins.).
Il Posto (United Artists; 86 mins.).

Shorts:

Time Out of War (British Film Institute, 23 mins.).
Coalface (British Film Institute, 10 mins.).

A ten-minute extract from *Il Posto* is available from the British Film Institute. This is a good starting-point for discussion on careers prospects, hopes for the future and boy–girl relationships.

The Education Department of the British Film Institute, 81 Dean Street, W1V 6AA, provides comprehensive lists of films available for teachers wishing to run courses in film appreciation or to use extracts for discussion purposes. For schools which become educational corporate members of the British Film Institute (£4. 0. 0. p.a.) a number of extracts from full-length features are available on hire from the central booking agency. There are also film study units on various themes—e.g. 'war on the screen', 'young people', 'silent comedy'.

Conclusion

STEPHEN TUNNICLIFFE

One of the more reassuring things about this collection of essays is the extent to which its contributors, highly individual though they are, think alike. There has, in the nature of things, been little close liaison between the English teachers concerned. We live far apart, and are heavily engaged in our separate schools. Indeed, when Geoffrey Summerfield first conceived the idea of the book he assumed that a considerable amount of elision and re-arrangement of the material would be inevitable. The schools, after all, differ in almost every way, size, traditions, personnel, educational emphasis. Yet again and again we find ourselves as English teachers facing the same problems in the same ways; so that the statements both complement and reinforce one another. It should be evident to any reader that we do not, however, subscribe to the notion of a new orthodoxy in English teaching, however enlightened. Our statements of the way we go about our work are presented, in Geoffrey Summerfield's phrase, as 'an offering to a conversation'—an attempt to promote and extend that 'meaningful dialogue' which lies at the heart of all good English teaching.

It would be misleading, however, to overemphasize our similarities. British readers will recognize more readily than those overseas the differences that spring from the different functions of the six schools represented here. We feel that such variety adds to the value of the symposium by showing that wide differences of scope and environment do not preclude a common pursuit of articulateness. Leeds Modern School and Manchester Grammar School, with their fairly clearly defined traditions and functions, face different problems in their English work from the three comprehensive schools; and these in turn differ both from one another by virtue of their settings and their educational policies, and from the more selective technical high school, Dane Court. We have tried to clarify these differences in our introductory descriptions.

One of the first points arising from this set of statements concerns the idea of an English syllabus. Even the question 'syllabus or no syllabus?' remains an open one. Brian Phythian, working within the context of a highly organized, rigidly selective academic school, and benefiting from the natural homogeneity of a well-qualified graduate staff, can rely on a 'set of broad principles'. Anthony Adams too, in the less favourable academic climate of a large urban comprehensive school, prefers to concentrate on building up a close working relationship within the department through weekly meetings and teamwork. I, on the other hand, have chosen to attempt to clarify the English work by systematizing it within a syllabus. We are all, I suppose, aware of the dangers inherent in a set syllabus—ossification, a substitution of second-hand ideas for dynamic day-to-day discovery. On the other hand, my syllabus, Brian Phythian's set of principles applied by a homogeneous staff, Anthony Adams' team-teaching and continuous dialogue are all aiming at the same thing, a purposeful continuity and sense of direction in the English work.

The tendency towards developing English work through topics and themes rather than fragmenting it into areas of study, and the consequent moving away from course-books of the traditional kind, accentuates the problem of achieving continuity. Anthony Adams relies on 'a department policy of linking the kind of project studied with the development and maturation of the pupils'; I attempt to control it by suggesting a 'framework of experience' from which themes should be chosen. I suspect that this problem will be greater in the comprehensive schools, which are in the process of building up an identity, than in establishments like Manchester Grammar School with clearly defined functions and objectives. It may be that it will not finally be resolved until the curriculum changes hinted at in such experiments as the one at Dane Court have re-shaped our whole concept of the purpose of state secondary schools. The extent to which this is at present in the melting-pot is well illustrated by two recent contributions to the current dialogue on secondary education. Frank Musgrove, in advocating placing the teacher 'in a proper contractual relationship with his clients' the parents, stresses the need for divergence and variety of individual choice. 'There is no more fatal blow to English liberty', he says, 'than the area comprehensive school.'[1] On the other hand Cyril Poster sees the area school as a valuable antidote to the less desirable aspects of a materialistic society. 'Within the currently changing pattern of education may well lie the answer to the rootlessness and aimlessness of much of modern living. The comprehensive school must almost of necessity be a community school.'[2] This controversy may seem far removed from the teaching of English. I believe, nevertheless, that the approach demonstrated in these essays, with its emphasis on person-to-person contact in the classroom, and heuristic, individualistic discovery, constitutes a valuable contribution to the whole educational debate.

It is no accident that every one of these essays places considerable weight on qualities of individual personality. Five years ago Frank Whitehead chose as the title of his book on English teaching that vivid phrase 'the disappearing dais'. If we accept the approach advocated in his book, and given substance by the practitioners here, the dais and the remote authoritarian attitudes it implies have indeed disappeared. Irene Summerbell points out the initial step towards creating a learning situation: 'As a starting-point we must accept the validity of [the

[1] F. Musgrove and P. H. Taylor, *Society and the Teacher's Role* (1969), p. 86.

[2] 'The Head and the Community School', in *Headship in the 1970s*, ed. B. Allen (1968), p. 64.

children's] experience.' From here we move naturally to 'an awareness of their own and other people's feelings, wants and interests' (Graham White). As English work develops through discussion, analysis, creative expression in all its forms, in the pursuit of topics or the development of projects, this touchstone of an awareness of and respect for the individual remains vital—even to the extent of deciding the form of expression. 'For the teacher to insist on determining the form is to risk the pupil falsifying: to say *what* he wants he must be able to say it *how* he wishes' (Robert Shaw).

That this approach places great strain on the teachers implementing it is undeniable. No English teacher can 'switch off' at the end of a lesson, even at the end of a day or week, and all experienced English teachers are only too familiar with that sense of emotional and spiritual bombardment that gives rise to restless nights and distracted days at the end of a school term. And it is not merely what one might call this emotional 'metal fatigue' that makes the teaching of English along these lines so exhausting. There is also the extent to which one has constantly to be a source of new ideas, new slants, new media, different aspects of themes, different literary sources and parallels. This is well illustrated by Graham White's reaching out in all directions in following up and expanding themes like 'mining', 'food', even 'school'; or by Irene Summerbell's description of the range of activities—taped discussions, interviews, collections of photographs, social surveys—entered into on the English side of her integrated Twentieth-century Studies course. The need for such varied and wide-ranging approaches carries implications relating not merely to the kind of training English teachers should have—though I certainly do not underestimate the need for reform here, stated so pungently in Geoffrey Summerfield's introduction—but to the whole question of in-service refreshment and 're-charging of batteries'. Brian Phythian's 'national staff college of English' would be one way of providing it. Others might be to use the teacher's centres, as Graham White suggests, or to develop a policy of exchanges between schools and teacher-training establishments, or to encourage regular secondment of practising teachers. The pressure of work in school, while undoubtedly a stimulus to a good teacher, does tend to isolate the schools from one another. It is as much as one can do to find time during term to meet one's own English staff, as these essays testify; a determined policy on the part of the colleges and departments of education is needed to further that fruitful exchange of ideas which as English teachers we all need.

In spite of the wilder pronouncements of Marshall McLuhan we still, as a whole, rely on literature as a central source in English teaching. Enough is said here about different media and methods, and about the stress placed on 'oracy', to defend us from Robert Shaw's suggestion that English teachers are 'print obsessed'. As he himself points out, we need the rich resources of literature both as a 'storehouse of values' and as a starter or springboard for individual expression; we need, too, to teach reading, whether, like Brian Phythian, we can rely on a literate book-conscious home background, or whether we have to provide at school the bulk of our pupils' literary experience—much of it probably through paperbacks—like Graham White at Settle and Anthony Adams at West Bromwich, both serving what we may be tempted to call, in one sense, culturally deprived areas. At all times we have to rely too on our own wide and widening range of literary experience. The essays here provide convincing evidence that no cultural butterfly, Sunday-paper skimmer, is likely to find himself well-equipped to teach English in schools. Extensive, continuous, discriminating reading provides the ground-swell of an English teacher's professional life, and informs his teaching at every level.

There is a danger, however, that even when our teaching

deploys and is aware of the multifarious richness of the different media of communication the external examinations by which our pupils are assessed will remain 'print obsessed'. There is a general movement away from internal English examinations by the writers of this book; but all of us are still bound by the G.C.E. and C.S.E. examinations, and the former, especially the notorious yet still almost universal O-level language paper, depends almost entirely on a restricted range of literary skills. Even the J.M.B. experiment in school assessment for this examination, now summarized in their circular EP 1 (April 1969), can leave little room, as Robert Shaw shows, for any other forms of English expression. This may be due partly to the inexperience and initial timidity of the teachers implementing it. The method does at least ensure a more realistic relation between what is done in the classroom and what 'the world' accepts as competence in English, and for this reason alone we look forward hopefully to its extension. At a more academic level the A-level English literature examination is also unsatisfactory, encouraging what Brian Phythian calls 'the regurgitation of opinions' and leading at worst to narrow stereotyped teaching. It is no wonder that English teachers outside the grammar schools are backing the more flexible C.S.E., with its emphasis on school-based syllabuses and assessments. Once again the need is clear for some national—or even regional—English forum, this time both for clarifying the relations between different schools' examining methods when they are school-based, and as a means of bridging what Phythian calls 'the great gulf which exists between enlightened teachers and some professional examiners'.

We are suspicious, then, of the monolithic, impersonal structure of external English examinations. I hope this does not suggest that we are prepared to lower our standards of expression in the pursuit of a sloppily liberal English curriculum. It should be evident that none of the contributors would condone this, or is unaware of the need for accuracy and precision as well as fluency, whether in conducting an interview, writing a poem or writing up an experiment. We *are* aware that command, control of language is not simply a matter of learning rules. 'Formal'—i.e. Latinate—English grammar died an unlamented death some years ago when it was realized how little, if at all, such artificial manipulation of patterns affected true literacy, and how pernicious its side-effects were—the inhibition of that copiousness which alone leads to mastery being not the least of them. English teachers now tend to deal with questions of mechanical accuracy and coherent expression as they arise, on an individual basis. The problem, as always, is how to make the opportunities for such individual language 'surgeries' —to use Brian Phythian's expression. The emphasis given in this book to group and individual projects and group rather than class discussions makes this less difficult than it might be in a more traditional class teaching situation. Moreover, where English expression, in whatever form, is directed realistically towards communicating, often with a peer-group, its effectiveness can be and usually is checked empirically *in situ*. Often the blank incomprehension of a child's classroom audience is a more salutary corrective to his expression than an ocean of red ink.

Having cleared ourselves of the aridities of formal grammar we are perhaps unduly reluctant to accept the need for linguistic studies in school. One cannot ignore the significant contribution to knowledge of this comparatively young science in recent times, especially in the fields of comparative and social linguistics. Undoubtedly this will be reflected in the universities, and we will be welcoming more linguistics 'specialists' to the schools. It may be that Geoffrey Summerfield's pointers to the applications of linguistic studies in the schools are the right ones. In any case, the fact that two of the six schools here are developing language studies in the sixth form, and that one of them, Churchfields, is taking part in the Schools Council Linguistics Project, shows that we are open-minded and receptive on this issue.

In our separate essays we have tried to achieve a balance between what we feel approximates to the ideal teaching situation and what we actually practise at present. This is difficult, and we may at times have been over-optimistic about the extent to which we have succeeded, within the familiar chalky, ink-stained, battered surroundings, in creating a purposeful learning environment. If English teachers often seem like rebels in school it is because they react so strongly against the hidebound rigidity of so much that goes on in secondary schools. Has the 'standard classroom' in fact changed much over the last fifty years? Does not every detail of it, from its battered uncomfortable hideous desks—still all lined up in one direction in the vast majority of cases—to its tatty notice-board and dominating blackboard, reinforce the hierarchical, compartmentalized pattern of secondary education, where 'subjects' jostle one another for precedence, English among them, and where staff meetings so often degenerate into degrading squabbles about status? No wonder we are reaching out in all directions from this prison: seeking new media of expression—films, sound collage on tape, improvized drama; striving to convert our surroundings, if only by re-grouping desks, as Anthony Adams does, and replacing them by chairs and tables, into more attractive work-centres; building up our own store-houses of materials—pictures, duplicated extracts, 'found' objects, magazines, Sellotape. No wonder, too, that one of the most frequent *cris de coeur* is for secretarial assistance and equipment, a duplicator or photocopier, and a more enlightened view from the administrators of what properly constitutes 'English' material. In so far as the mother-tongue is the chief medium of our civilization and culture it is as wide as life itself, and the English classroom should at least hint at the richness and variety of life, and provide as far as possible a microcosm of the outside world rather than a cell isolated from it.

But this is a bigger matter really than providing suitable materials and environment or seeing that tape-recorders and ciné-cameras are not regarded as luxuries, important though this is in the present day-to-day business of teaching English. It calls in question the whole traditional structure of secondary education. It is for this reason that the last essay here describes not merely a scheme of work for English but an integrated course linking three subject disciplines. In this kind of scheme, in projects such as the integrated General Studies courses in many sixth forms on lines similar to the one I describe at Newtown, in positive liaison and collaboration such as Robert Shaw's with the Chemistry Department at Leeds Modern, lie the seeds of new growth in secondary education. As we in the schools reformulate our jobs to take account of the changing functions of education in today's and tomorrow's world it should be evident that the best English teaching will be in the lead. Touching life, as it does, at every point, the English Department is involved in so many of the humanizing activities that make a school more than a teaching machine—school newspapers, magazines, play-reading groups, 'theatre workshops' and play production, debating societies, writers' groups, libraries, visits and excursions.

This volume by practitioners on 'the front line', as Geoffrey Summerfield puts it, 'where the real questions are asked and where practical answers have expeditiously to be found', is both a contribution to the current educational debate and a statement of faith. Our justification and our rewards lie in the responses we evoke and the feed-back we receive from our pupils. It is their bubbling vitality, their eternal, exhausting, insatiable curiosity that even while it drains our energy provides the stimulus for such a book as this. It is to our pupils, therefore, past, present and to come, that we dedicate this work.

Glossary

Note. Children in Great Britain normally enter state *primary schools* at the age of five. When they are eleven (twelve in Scotland) they transfer to a *secondary school*, of which there are several different types. They remain at school until they are at least fifteen; the school-leaving age is to be raised to sixteen in 1972. If they decide to continue their education beyond the compulsory age they normally sit either the *General Certificate of Education* (G.C.E.) or the *Certificate of Secondary Education* (C.S.E.) before leaving the secondary school. Independent schools provide an alternative to state secondary education for those who can afford to pay the fees required. These include the *public schools*, many of them famous, richly endowed and with long traditions. Children normally enter these from fee-paying *preparatory schools* at the age of thirteen. (See also *direct grant schools*.)

A-level, see G.C.E.

Assembly: the name given to the daily morning meeting of the whole school, which must include, by law, a collective act of worship.

B.B.C. School Broadcasts: the state controlled British Broadcasting Corporation provides a wide variety of educational programmes both on radio and television.

British Film Institute: provides a valuable educational service, and information about films to schools (81 Dean Street, London, W1V 6AA).

Catchment area: secondary schools frequently serve a clearly defined geographical area, drawing all or most of their pupils from within it. This is more true of *comprehensive* schools than of the *selective* schools.

Chief Education Officer: the administrative head of a local education authority.

Colleges of Education: formerly called training colleges, these provide professional education, by means of three- or four-year courses, for the majority of the teaching profession.

Colleges of Further Education: locally-based colleges providing a variety of academic and vocational courses, many of them part-time, for those who have left school.

Comprehensive Schools: secondary schools that cater for the full ability-range. Most are co-educational, but there are some single sex comprehensive schools.

Course work: work carried out as a normal part of the curriculum. It is often used for assessment purposes in C.S.E. and G.C.E. examinations.

Creaming: the process whereby pupils of high ability in an area are directed towards a selective school (usually a grammar school) to the detriment of a competing comprehensive school.

Crowther Report (1959): a government-sponsored report on the education of boys and girls between the ages of fifteen and eighteen, under the chairmanship of Sir Geoffrey Crowther. The report recommended, among other things, the raising of the school-leaving age to sixteen in 1968 and less specialization in sixth-form education.

C.S.E., Certificate of Secondary Education: a certificate of attainment for less academic pupils than those taking G.C.E. O-level in secondary schools. Its scope is largely controlled by the teachers, especially under *Mode* 3, in which form the syllabus is planned, and tests are set and marked within the schools, subject to external moderation.

Department of Education and Science (D.E.S.): the government department responsible, under the Minister for Education and Science, for educational matters. It is the successor to the Ministry of Education and the Ministry of Science, which were merged in 1964. The department sets minimum standards of educational provision, controls educational building, the supply and training of teachers, and matters involving local educational authorities, but does *not* run schools or colleges, engage teachers, or prescribe curricula.

Direct Grant schools: secondary schools that are independent of the local education authority, receiving grants-in-aid direct from the Department of Education and Science on condition that they make twenty-five percent of their places available to pupils who have spent at least two years in a state school. They are mostly grammar schools, some of ancient foundation.

Director of Education, see Chief Education Officer.

Education Committees: voluntary bodies of elected and co-opted members responsible for running (through the Chief Education Officer and a large staff) schools in the area of a local education authority.

Eleven-plus: the name loosely applied to any method of selecting children at the end of their primary schooling for different types of secondary school. Tests normally include an assessment of intelligence, and of ability in English and Mathematics.

Entry: when used as in 'three-form entry' it is an indication of size of secondary school; a 'form' usually consists of 30 pupils and thus a three-form entry school would admit about 90 pupils from primary schools each year.

Examinations: internal examinations are set annually or more frequently in most secondary schools as a means of internal assessment; external examinations are the G.C.E. and C.S.E.

Examining Boards: the G.C.E. and C.S.E. examinations are administered by eight examining boards which have different syllabuses and set their own examinations (see N.U.J.M.B., W.J.E.C.). Control over standards is exercised by the *Schools Council for the Curriculum and Examinations.*

Fourth-year leavers: pupils who choose to leave school on reaching the minimum leaving age—at present fifteen. They are often reluctant students, and often leave without any form of certificate of attainment.

G.C.E., the General Certificate of Education: awarded in England and Wales by the eight examining boards. The Ordinary Level (O-level) examination is taken at about sixteen and a good performance is essential for admission to many careers. The Advanced Level (A-level), taken at about eighteen after two years in the sixth form, usually in three (but sometimes only in two) related subjects, provides the basis for admission to universities and colleges. In English there are two examinations at Ordinary Level, one in *English literature*, the other in *English language*. The A-level English examination is in literature only.

General Studies: usually applied to non-specialist studies in the sixth form, often involving liaison between different specialist subjects.

Grammar schools: selective secondary schools catering for more academically able pupils, and providing courses leading to the universities and colleges of education.

Head of English Department: teacher responsible for planning and organizing English teaching in a secondary school. He earns more for the responsibility, but often there is no specific secretarial assistance or reduction of teaching load.

H.M.C., Headmasters' Conference: an association formed by the independent (fee-paying) schools. The conference has powers to invite headmasters from state schools to join it.

H.M.I., Her Majesty's Inspectors of Schools: responsible for advising the schools, for maintaining standards, and for providing a link between local education authorities and the government ministries responsible for education.

Honours Degrees: British universities usually award degrees at honours and at general levels, the latter requiring a broader spread of studies but less depth. General degree courses are declining in importance. They are being replaced by general honours degrees in which two or three subjects are taken together in a combined honours course. Prospective teachers strive for an honours degree rather than a general degree because it is at present rewarded by a special allowance in their salary.

Houses: divisions or groupings in secondary schools *vertically*, i.e. covering the whole age range. They facilitate organization within the schools, and provide the structure for competitive games, and for pastoral tutor-groups cutting across form or ability groups. Housemasters or housemistresses are usually appointed to administer them, under the head of the school.

Housing estate: usually refers to houses owned by a local government body and let to working-class tenants, often at subsidized rents.

Junior Technical School *or* College: the 1944 Education Act made provision for technical schools as well as the better-known grammar and modern schools. They were termed *junior* to differentiate them from technical colleges, which were further education establishments.

L.E.A., Local Education Authority: responsible for ensuring that adequate provision is made in their area for primary and secondary education. They provide grants for pupils seeking higher education and facilities for further education in their area.

Maintained schools: financed wholly out of public funds, and not by fees or voluntary bodies.

Meals: school meals are provided below cost to pupils. Teachers have objected to administering this service, and L.E.A.s now employ ancillary staff for the purpose.

Middle school: (*a*) the term loosely applied to third- and fourth-year (13 to 15-year old) pupils in a secondary school; (*b*) a school catering for the age-range 9 to 13 or 14.

Milk: one-third of a pint daily is provided free to all primary school children who wish to have it; this service used to be provided in secondary schools.

Mixed ability: there is a move in many comprehensive schools towards teaching pupils in groups covering the whole ability range, rather than *streaming* them.

Mixed School: co-educational school.

Moderation: a method of ensuring parity of standards in national examinations, especially the C.S.E., when they are assessed within the schools. An outside *moderator*, usually a teacher from another school, makes his own assessment of a sample cross-section of the work, and advises on the marking scale to be used.

N.A.T.E., National Association for the Teaching of English (5 Imperial Road, Edgerton, Huddersfield, Yorkshire).

N.C.T.E., National Council of Teachers of English (508 South Sixth Street, Champaign, Illinois, U.S.A.).

Newsom Report (1963): a report by the Central Advisory Council for Education, on the education between the ages of thirteen and sixteen of pupils of average and less than average ability. The chairman was Mr (now Sir) John Newsom, and the report was entitled *Half our Future*. It recommended, among other things, the raising of the school-leaving age to sixteen in 1965, and resistance by the schools to external pressures for extending public examinations to pupils for whom they are inappropriate.

Non-specialist sixth form: sixth-form pupils normally follow a highly specialized curriculum based on two or three subjects, all related to 'arts' or 'sciences'. There have been repeated attempts to mitigate this evil by developing a range of General Studies courses to cover other subjects.

Nuffield Projects: the Nuffield Foundation (Nuffield Lodge, Regent's Park, London, N.W.1) has initiated a number of curriculum development projects in schools, notably in Science, Mathematics and Modern Languages.

N.U.J.M.B., Northern Universities Joint Matriculation Board: one of the biggest examining bodies, set up jointly by a group of universities. They have made considerable progress in a project for school assessment of the English language paper in the G.C.E. O-level examination.

O-level, the Ordinary level of the G.C.E. examination: normally 8 or 9 subjects are examined at the end of the fifth year in secondary schools, i.e. at the age of sixteen. A pass in 4 or 5 subjects is often the minimum qualification for entering academic courses in sixth forms. Passes in specific subjects at O-level may be required as a qualification for further education or for professional qualifications of many kinds.

Oxbridge: a portmanteau word for the universities of Oxford and Cambridge.

Preparatory school: independent fee-paying school in which the curriculum is directed towards the *common entrance* examination for public schools, taken at the age of thirteen.

Primary schools: state schools covering the age-range 5 to 11. They are normally divided into *infants* (5 to 7) and *junior* (8 to 11).

Public schools: a misleading name applied to a large number of independent fee-paying schools (usually boarding schools) for pupils of thirteen and over. See H.M.C.

R.S.L.A., raising the school-leaving age: legislation has been passed raising the age of compulsory schooling to sixteen; this will take effect in 1972.

'Scholarship boy': a term—less common now—for a boy who at the end of primary school (11+) gains a place in a selective secondary school, usually a grammar school.

Scholarship (examination) paper: special papers are set alongside the Advanced Level G.C.E. papers for pupils seeking admission to university. They will normally sit only one special paper, in the subject they intend to read at university.

Schools Council for the Curriculum and Examinations: set up in 1964 to bring together representatives of all parts of the education system. The council sets up research teams, curriculum development projects, publishes working papers and reports, and helps to found local *teachers' centres.*

Secondary Modern Schools: non-selective schools catering for the majority of secondary pupils. They were intended to have 'parity of esteem' with selective schools, but the social effect of selection at 11+ has been to devalue the modern schools. Many are now being re-organized as comprehensive schools.

Setting: many secondary schools 'set' their pupils according to ability in different subjects. Sets thus become the teaching units rather than classes or forms. See also *streaming*.

Sixth form: the top age-group in grammar and comprehensive schools, catering for pupils aged from sixteen to eighteen or nineteen. It is usually organized in two year-groups, *lower* (or (first-year) and *upper* (or second-year). Big schools may have a third-year sixth as well.

Sixth Form College (Junior College): some L.E.A.s are planning comprehensive education so as to provide a transfer at the school-leaving age of sixteen to a tertiary stage, the sixth form college.

Speech Day: traditionally the annual occasion on which a secondary school publicly takes stock of its progress and achievements. Parents and other guests, including a distinguished guest speaker, are invited and prizes are often presented to pupils. This is the formal highlight of the school's year.

Streaming: a method of sorting secondary (and occasionally primary) pupils into teaching groups according to academic ability. It has been widely criticized, but remains the most usual method in secondary schools.

Teachers' centres: local centres set up under the aegis of the Schools Council to encourage discussion and liaison among practising teachers.

Thorne scheme: a method of selection at 11+ initiated in Thorne, Yorkshire. Under the scheme only border-line candidates for selective schools are assessed outside the primary school itself.

Times Educational Supplement: national weekly journal devoted to educational matters. It offers the most complete advertising service for teachers' posts.

Use of English: (*a*) an examination at A-level instigated by the universities. It has met with considerable opposition from English teachers; (*b*) an influential independent quarterly journal at present edited by F. Whitehead and C. Parry and published by Chatto and Windus, 40 William IV Street, London, W.C.2.

W.J.E.C., Welsh Joint Education Committee: the body responsible for national examinations in Wales.

Bibliography

GENERAL

Barnes, Douglas, James Britton, *et al. Language, the Learner and the School.* Penguin Books, 1969.

Bolt, Sydney. *The Right Response.* Hutchinson, 1966.

Britton, James (ed.). *Talking and Writing.* Methuen, 1967.

Dixon, John. *Growth through English.* O.U.P., 1969.

Flower, F. D. *Language and Education.* Longmans, 1966.

Harding, D. W. *Experience into Words.* Chatto and Windus, 1963.

Holbrook, David. *English for Maturity.* C.U.P., 2nd rev. ed., 1967.

Jackson, Brian (ed.). *English versus Examinations.* Chatto and Windus, 1965.

Lawton, D. *Social Class, Language and Education.* Routledge, 1968.

Lenneberg, E. H. (ed.). *New Directions in the Study of Language.* M.I.T. Press, 1964.

Manvell, Roger. *The Living Screen.* Harrap, 1961.

Marland, Michael. *Towards the New Fifth: English and the Humanities for the Young School Leaver.* Longmans, 1969.

Musgrove, Frank, and Philip H. Taylor. *Society and the Teacher's Role.* Routledge, 1969.

Northern Universities Joint Matriculation Board (circulars on school-assessing available, free, from N.U.J.M.B., Manchester):

General Certificate of Education: Experimental Scheme of School Assessment in English Language (Ordinary). Circular EP 1, April 1969.

Hewitt, E. A. *The Reliability of G.C.E. O-level Examinations in English Language.* Circular OP 27, August 1967.

Hewitt, E. A., and D. I. Gordon. *English Language: an Experiment in School Assessing (First Interim Report).* Circular OP 22, December 1965.

Petch, J. A. *English Language: an Experiment in Assessing (Second Interim Report).* Circular OP 26, July 1967.

Poster, Cyril. 'The head and the community school' in *Headship in the 1970s*, edited by B. Allen. Blackwell, 1968.

Quirk, Randolph (ed.). *The Use of English.* 2nd ed., Longmans, 1968.

Sapir, Edward. *Language.* Hart-Davis, 1963.

Culture, Language and Personality. University of Columbia Press, 1966.

Steiner, George. *Language and Silence.* Faber, 1967.

Stuart, Simon. *Say: an Experiment in Learning.* Nelson, 1969.

Summerfield, Geoffrey. *Topics in English.* Batsford, 1965.

(ed.) *Creativity in English.* N.C.T.E., 1968.

Thompson, Denys (ed.). *Directions in the Teaching of English.* C.U.P., 1969.

Whitehead, Frank. *The Disappearing Dais.* Chatto and Windus, 1966.

Whorf, Benjamin L. *Language, Thought and Reality.* M.I.T. Press, 1956.

Wilkinson, Andrew (ed.). 'The Place of Language', in *Educational Review*, vol. 20, no. 2. University of Birmingham School of Education, 1968.

Williams, Raymond. *The Long Revolution.* Penguin Books, 1965.

FOR CLASSROOM USE

Adland, P. *Group Approach to Drama.* Longmans, 1964–7 (Books 1–4).

Bartlett, P., and E. Bates. *Impetus.* Ginn, 1969.

B.B.C. Publications: *Listening and Writing* and *Living Language.*

Brimer, A. (ed.). *Bristol Achievement Tests.* Nelson, 1969.

Dixon, John, Leslie Stratta, *et al. Reflections.* O.U.P., 1963.

Hodgson, John, and Ernest Richards. *Living Expression*, 2 vols and teachers' book (*Experience and Expression*). Ginn, 1968.

Mabey, Richard (ed.). *Connexions.* Penguin Books, 1969– .

Marland, Michael. *Pictures for Writing.* Blackie, 1966.

More Pictures for Writing. Blackie, 1969.

Middleton, R. G. *Senior Spelling.* Methuen, 1966.

Mittins, W. H. *A Grammar of Modern English.* Methuen, 1962.

Poole, R. H., and P. J. Shepherd. *Impact*, 2 vols and teachers' book. Heinemann, 1967.

Bibliography

Summerfield, Geoffrey. *Voices*, 3 vols and teachers' book. Penguin Books, 1968.

Thompson, Arnold, Peter Jefferson and Brian Derbyshire. *English First*. 4 vols, University Tutorial Press, 1968– .

Index

Index